THE *ART* OF LEAP FROGGING

Maher Kaddoura

ISBN: 979-8-9895094-2-3

Dedicated to my late son Hikmat

CONTENTS

An anthology of stories and wisdom from great people who have identified innovations, and applied methods and tools to reduce the time and effort it takes to achieve great outcomes.

Leapfrogging is the small improvement leading to quantum leaps.

MAHER KADDOURA

A symbol of boundless resilience, Maher Kaddoura's journey paints an awe-inspiring panorama of human potential. His life story, interwoven with diverse cultures, spiritual roots, and a steadfast commitment to humanity, is an anthem of ingenuity. A transformative leader, Maher has adeptly utilized his experiences and passions to craft a lasting, positive legacy for the world.

NURTURED BY DIVERSITY:
MAHER KADDOURA'S CULTURAL UPBRINGING

Born into a rich Jordanian and Palestinian heritage, Maher was raised in a Muslim family, while his academic education was shaped in a Catholic school. This intriguing blend of cultures and religions fostered a broader perspective in Maher. The ability to look beyond societal labels and focus on the shared bonds of humanity became his early hallmark.

During his adolescence, Maher's character was formed by three transformative experiences that later served as navigational beacons in his adult life. The Boy Scouts instilled in him the ethos of community service, while his early business ventures in selling his mother's used items kindled his entrepreneurial spirit. A sleeping bag gift from his wandering cousin at 15 years ignited an unquenchable thirst for exploration.

These experiences facilitated the crystallization of Maher's three overriding passions: philanthropy, entrepreneurship, and global exploration. The early recognition of these passions during his university tenure symbolized Maher's first "leapfrog moment," a defining phase that laid a robust foundation for his future endeavors.

BALANCING PASSION AND DISCIPLINE: CARVING OUT A MEANINGFUL LIFE

As I reflect on my journey, I recall being guided by an intense passion that led me to study Civil Engineering at Nottingham University-UK. However, my fascination gradually shifted towards the managerial aspects of the field grounded in an engineering mindset, which then led me to take up leadership roles post-graduation.

Joining a unique and very challenging project at what is called Accenture was a turning point in my career, opening up a new realm of discipline and structure. This venture helped me realize an important life lesson that became my guiding mantra: "Passion inspires, discipline delivers." With this principle in mind, I felt prepared to chart my path.

WELCOMING CHANGE WITH OPEN ARMS: STEERING THROUGH LIFE'S OBSTACLES

Years of hard work paid off when I relocated to Chicago, marking the beginning of my professional journey as a programmer with Accenture. My dedication and growing expertise led to my rise as a Managing Partner, a role in which I was entrusted with the task of expanding the company's Middle East practice.

I never allowed my thirst for knowledge to be quenched. I was always seeking new challenges and continuously ascending the learning curve. After 18 enriching years with Accenture, I decided to embark on a new journey, launching a series of successful consulting firms, always keen to adapt, transform, and tackle challenges head-on.

BOUNCING FORWARD FROM HEARTBREAK: TRANSFORMING SORROW INTO A BEACON OF HOPE

Beneath my jovial demeanor and vibrant personality lies a painful chapter of personal loss. The tragic hit-and-run incident that claimed my 17-year-old son Hikmat's life plunged me into a period of deep grief. Despite the pain, I mustered exceptional resilience and channelled my sorrow into a force for good by initiating the Hikmat Road Safety Program, thereby transforming a personal tragedy into a beacon of hope.

THE GLOBAL EXPLORER: EMBARKING ON ADVENTURES AROUND THE WORLD

I have an unyielding zest for adventure that has led me across 90 countries and 250 cities, from the snowy peaks of Mount Everest to the ancient Incan ruins of Machu Picchu, from the icy landscapes of the North Pole to the scenic vistas of the Ring of Kerry. I believe travel is a powerful tool to broaden perspectives, instigate personal growth, and foster a global understanding of diversity.

SHARING WISDOM GLOBALLY: THE GIFT OF KNOWLEDGE KEEPS GIVING

Blessed with a rich reservoir of wisdom, I'm committed to sharing my insights and contributing towards positive global change. My strong belief in collaboration and empirical knowledge is at the heart of my mission to enhance lives. This commitment is demonstrated through my various roles as a consultant, motivational speaker, author, and philanthropist.

EMBRACING THE FULLNESS OF LIFE: LIVING THE 86400 SECONDS

Inspired by the profound words of Kahlil Gibran, "Don't live half a life," I've absorbed the essence of living every one of the 86400 seconds in a day to its fullest potential. I believe fearlessness, imagination, and audacious goals form the cornerstone of a fulfilling life. True living begins at the brink of our comfort zones, the magical realm where we start tapping into our highest potential.

CREATING A LEAPFROG MOVEMENT AROUND THE WORLD

Building on my personal "leapfrog moments," I am committed to sparking similar leaps in others across the globe. I believe these pivotal moments of realization and transformation can drive humanity towards a brighter, more prosperous future. I aim to initiate a worldwide leapfrog movement, igniting change and inspiring individuals to surpass their limitations, thereby contributing to a better world.

LEAVING A LASTING IMPRESSION: INSPIRING THROUGH LEGACY

Looking back on my remarkable journey and the numerous lives I've had the privilege to positively influence, I am dedicated to creating an enduring legacy of inspiration and empowerment. I hope my story will serve as a shining testament to the power of passion, resilience, and the transformative power of human connection.

LIFE ACCORDING TO MAHER

"Passion inspires, discipline delivers" - a powerful life lesson that became my guiding mantra."

"I was always seeking new challenges and continuously ascending the learning curve."

"Despite the pain, I mustered exceptional resilience and channelled my sorrow into a force for good."

"I believe travel is a powerful tool to broaden perspectives, instigate personal growth, and foster a global understanding of diversity."

"I've absorbed the essence of living every one of the 86400 seconds in a day to its fullest potential."

"True living begins at the brink of our comfort zones, the magical realm where we start tapping into our highest potential."

"I aim to initiate a worldwide leapfrog movement, igniting change and inspiring individuals to surpass their limitations."

The Art of Leapfrogging

MAHER KADDOURA

Management Consultant, a Serial Entrepreneur, Angel Investor, Social Change Maker, Public Speaker and Adventurer

Maher Kaddoura's psyche has developed through an eclectic mix of heritage and spirituality. As a Jordanian, he is also a proud Palestinian by descent, and a muslim who studied at a catholic school. This potentially conflicting mix, has in fact resulted in a tolerant, reflective individual who looks beyond labels to see humanity.

Maher's philanthropy has been a testament to his focus on humankind, with a diverse and imaginative range of projects rooted in the concept of helping people. Whether it's from a voluntary basis, as a consultant, motivational speaker or author, Maher believes "unconditional giving elevates yourself."

Whilst growing up Maher had 3 main experiences which shaped his adult life. As a boy scout the concept of volunteering and helping others became embedded in his persona. His naturally altruistic nature was given an outlet with the premise to 'serve society' encapsulated by the scouts. Charity was certainly

"Passion inspires, discipline delivers."

a passion, but he also found a taste for entrepreneurship and making money. By selling his mother's used bits and pieces, he started to appreciate how satisfying business could be. Then, at 15 years old he was given a sleeping bag by a nomadic cousin. Maher put it to good use and explored Europe, learning from different people and cultures.

"Unconditional giving elevates yourself."

Not many young people are fortunate enough to have found their passion by the time they reach university, but Maher had identified 3, charity, entrepreneurship and travel. It could be regarded as his first Leapfrog moment, getting to a point so early in his life that his passions paved the way for all his future endeavors.

With that in mind, he studied Civil Engineering at Nottingham University, but quickly understood that he much preferred the management side of the course. After getting his Degree, he took another course - in discipline, when he joined the US Army on a special project in Jordan. That lesson was to stay with him his whole life and provide him with the mantra he has today, 'passion inspires, discipline delivers'.

After 2 years in the army, Maher settled in Chicago where he initially worked for Accenture as a programmer. He later moved to Saudi Arabia as a Managing Partner and set up the Accenture Middle East practice. He likes a life of change and challenge, and gets bored if he's not moving up the learning curve, so after 18 years he left Accenture to start a number of very successful consulting firms.

Concealed beneath the abundant passion, energy and humor, is also a story of immense pain, extraordinary inner strength, and unyielding faith. In 2008, his 17 year old son Hikmat was killed in a hit and run incident in Jordan. Even at his lowest ebb, Maher's grief was put to good use, founding the Hikmat Road Safety Programme which entailed setting up walking areas, pedestrian crossings and safety barriers, and even building 1200 playgrounds to keep children off the streets.

Hopefully, Maher ditched his cousin's sleeping bag a while ago, but to date he has visited 90 countries, 250 cities, reached the summit of Mount Everest, and explored Machu Picchu, the North Pole and Ring of Kerry.

Today he looks forward to yet another adventure, as he establishes a project with the premise of sharing good ideas and good practices in a collaborative, democratized arena. In line with his benefactor objectives, he wants to share and exchange empirical knowledge which will undoubtedly have a positive impact on the world.

Maher in his own words...

DON'T LIVE HALF A LIFE

When I was about 11 years old my father shared with me a poem by Kahil Gibran who said "don't live half a life". At that time, the concept of living only half a life confused me, and in a way obsessed me. How can anyone live only half a life? As I grew older, the answer to that question became clearer, and I realized that in order to live a full life, you need to create your own story where you are the hero. Being a supporting actor or mere prop in someone else's story, is when you only live half your life.

Over half a century later, this idea of only living half a life has stayed with me and perhaps is the reason for me wanting to write this book. Because I want to help people be more successful in their personal and work life, so they can embrace their own personal journey, so they can live a full life in a story where they play the main part. Although, living a full life, with purpose and passion is not as easy as it sounds. You need to be fearless, be ready to experiment, to have imagination, and to have a goal bigger than yourself. Life starts at the edge of your comfort zone, and this is where the magic happens, this is where you begin to live a full life.

THE 'LUCKY ZONE'

My adoption of what I call the 'Lucky Zone' has been pivotal in both my personal advancement and business growth.

"Leapfrogging is a matter of reaching where you want to go, faster and with less effort."

It's where foresight, agility and action converge, enabling me to springboard ahead of competition and personal limits. Recognizing the 'Lucky Zone' as a space shaped by my own actions, where chance favors the connected and the prepared, I've learned to operate from a point where my initiatives can have the greatest effect.

On a personal level, increasing my awareness and presence has allowed me to capitalize on opportunities that once seemed fortuitous, but were actually created by my readiness to act. Professionally, this meant not just riding the wave of change, but often being the one to set it in motion. This active engagement with the forces of change has helped me turn the 'Lucky Zone' into a launchpad for leapfrogging to new heights, ensuring that my trajectory isn't just upward, but also forward, outpacing traditional pathways to success.

LEAPFROGGING

As an investor in education technology around the world, I do lots of philanthropic work related to technology, education, training and upskilling. I have a training and development company based in the UAE and Saudi Arabia, and it's a topic close to my heart. However, innovation is also very close to my heart, because it is at the heart of Leapfrogging. I am constantly trying to think about how we can create new paths and achieve more, even faster?

For me Leapfrogging is simply a matter of reaching where you want to go, faster and with less effort. Whether as an individual or a company, Leapfrogging is moving forward and upward, further and faster, to a destination, or state of progress which is sustainable. As an analogy, we all know the world needs less deforestation and more trees planted. A human being would probably only be capable of planting a few thousand trees a year, however, there are drone fleets right now which are planting 400,000 seeds per day. Not only that, it's possible to do a soil test to plant specific seeds which will thrive in certain soils. This is Leapfrogging, skipping a path, creating new paths, leveraging technology, ideas, and methods, inspiring people. And if you take this concept and start applying it to everything you do as an individual, and share your knowledge with others, you will be helping to create a Leapfrog Nation.

JUGAAD

The Urdu word 'Jugaad' comes to mind and is now in the Oxford English Dictionary as "A flexible approach to problem-solving that uses limited resources in an innovative way". And this is something I do on a daily basis, it's a kind of frugal innovation. So part of the book focuses on how I can bring more impact to people? That's why the idea of the book is to create a movement, a community of Leapfroggers around the world who believe in leapfrogging for the greater good of humanity. This book is to inspire people to do just that. Every individual reading it will be reflecting on it from their own unique perspective. For the book, I interviewed 30 people from all different walks of life, each with their

"If you've got a dream, you have to protect it. If people can't do something themselves, they'll tell you, you can't do it. If you want something, go and get it. Period."

own unique perspective and unique life stories, and I have learned something new from each of them, and I guarantee that readers will too. What follows is a selection of short narratives from some of the most inspirational people I have met, people who have used Leapfrogging as a tool, mindset, or better way of thinking.

86400

My book is part of my legacy to inspire and help people reflect on their own lives, and perhaps start to look at things with a different lens. I want to help people to feel energized, to feel able to jump out of bed every morning with a real sense of purpose and passion. Regardless of whether they want to be just happier, or have a great family life, or money, or a career etc.., I guarantee that this book will, in some way, help them achieve that. Because each day we are all given 86400 seconds, and what we do with those seconds is up to each individual. I want this book to inspire people, young and old to make the most of those seconds.

REFLECTION

As I reach my 65th year, I look back on Gibran's poem and can reflect on my full life. I can say I have not had half a love, or entertained half friends. I have neither pampered those with half a talent, or accepted only half a solution. I have had, and am having an action packed life. A life full of charitable deeds, professional success and travel. A life noted for its social impact, and the people it has affected. A life full of love and friendship, but also marred with pain and loss. A spiritual life, a life of comedy and tragedy, drama and thrills. I have not lived half a life, and the best is yet to come.

To see more on
Maher Kaddoura

TAP INTO CUTTING-EDGE TECHNOLOGIES

In our fast-paced, technology-driven world, we often find that the best way forward is not always a step-by-step progression, but a series of leaps and bounds. Harnessing the power of advanced technologies allows us to leap over traditional methods, carving out new pathways and making swift progress.

> *"Efficiency is doing better what is already being done."*
>
> *Peter Drucker*

Leapfrogging encourages us to acknowledge and employ these cutting-edge technologies to outpace conventional processes, construct new routes, and utilize impressive innovations to accelerate our advancement:

NATIONAL PROGRAMS

India's Aadhaar program offers a compelling example at a national level. This digital identity system leapfrogs over traditional paper-based identity verification, supplying a unique identifier to over a billion people, easing access to various services.

CORPORATES

Consider Amazon. It employs advanced AI and robotics in its warehouses to enhance productivity, leapfrogging over traditional manual warehousing methods.

NEW VENTURES AND STARTUPS

SpaceX, a pioneer in aerospace manufacturing and space transportation, is leveraging advanced technologies to circumvent traditional barriers in space exploration, aiming to make space travel more accessible and affordable.

LOCAL COMMUNITY CHANGE

At a community level, Kenya's M-Pesa provides an excellent example. It's a mobile phone-based money transfer service that leapfrogs over traditional banking hurdles, offering financial services to millions who previously had no access to banking.

INDIVIDUAL PERSONAL

An individual can use an AI-driven language-learning platform like Duolingo to learn new languages at their pace. This tool bypasses traditional language learning methods and provides a personalized, interactive, and accessible learning experience.

In our current era, marked by rapid technological advances, the ability to leverage these technologies is becoming increasingly critical. They are about redefining norms, overcoming boundaries, and catalyzing progress. As we embrace these technologies and adapt to their changes, we are not merely moving forward; we're leapfrogging.

JOSE M. HERNANDEZ

Speaker and President and CEO at
Tierra Luna Engineering, LLC

There are now 8 billion people living on Earth, but fewer than 600 have gone to space, a tiny fraction of the entire population, and José Hernández is one of them. In itself this is quite an incredible accomplishment, but it is not until we delve into José's childhood that we realize just how remarkable an achievement it is.

He had an inauspicious start to his education, spending most of his early childhood following his Mexican parents as they trailed across California state picking crops. Going from one school to another and spending the weekends harvesting in fields, meant that José did not speak English fluently until he was 12 years old. This made the prospect of joining NASA seem like a mere fantasy. But with the support of his parents, who refused to accept the destiny bestowed on their son, and an insightful teacher who noticed his hidden potential, José was given the chance to thrive, and he grabbed it with both hands.

After the teacher made a home visit to encourage José's parents to keep him in one school, the family settled in Stockton. With a more stable lifestyle, José developed a love of engineering, science, and math. Although his English had suffered from his nomadic lifestyle, these other subjects became his 'shelter' for their ability to circumvent language. In December 1972, when he was ten years old, José sat in front of his small TV and watched Eugene Cernan, the last man to walk on the moon. That day, José's destiny was set.

In a country often lost with its pursuit for immediate riches and fame, a little boy was inspired by an event happening 225,000 miles away. With hard work, determination, and perseverance, he followed his dream with the odds stacked against him, and he triumphed - a shining example of the American Dream!
Although José came from very humble beginnings, in a lot of ways, he was richer than most kids. His parents gave him more than money; they gave him their time. He remembers his parents sitting at the kitchen table while he completed his homework and believing in their little boy who looked up at the stars and dared to dream.

Eventually gaining a B.S. in electrical engineering and an M.S. in electrical and computer engineering, José worked for five years before first applying to NASA. This began a long battle between applications and rejections until he was finally accepted as an astronaut candidate on his twelfth application at the age of 41 years. It sounds straightforward, but it was José's relentless determination and analytical approach which shined through.

He left NASA in 2011, and since then, he has run for Congress, founded an educational charity, and has published three books, including a bilingual book called The Boy Who Touched the Stars. As a successful businessman, he commands an enthusiastic audience at his public speaking events. He is now based in California with his wife and their five children and, having already accomplished so much, he is living another dream by owning and, along with his father, farming a small vineyard. The name, Tierra Luna Cellars, is inspired from his view of the constellations from space. A man who has been to the moon and back, and yet sees his most important mission to leave mother earth and humanity better than when he found it.

"Always give more than people expect of you."

Jose in his own words...

THE KEY TO SUCCESS

I would introduce myself as a person who is not afraid to dream big, but who is also willing to put the work in to convert that dream into reality. Perhaps due to my upbringing, I have a strong work ethic and resilience. NASA rejected me not once, not twice, not even three or four times, but rather 11 times. It wasn't until the twelfth application that I was accepted. I think resilience, perseverance and hard work are my key ingredients for success in life.

LEAPFROGGING

My leapfrog moment came to me early on, when I first told my father that I wanted to be an astronaut. I was ten years old, and it was a cold Winter in 1972. I had just watched the Apollo 17 Mission and Astronaut Gene Cernan walking on the moon. After absorbing my rather ambitious announcement, my father sat me down at the kitchen table and gave me something invaluable. Before all else, he validated the dream, and then he told me to follow a 5-ingredient recipe.

• First, determine your purpose in life.
• Second, recognize your purpose and your goal and how far you are from reaching it.
• Third, draw yourself a roadmap so you know how to get there.
• Fourth, prepare yourself according to the challenge you choose.
• Fifth, that same effort you put in on weekends and seven days a week during summer picking crops, (he pointed to my books), you put that effort there.

Then you mix that up. That's the recipe to succeed.

His parting words that evening were "always give more than what people expect of you."

> "Going to space changed me, it changed my perspective of life on our planet."

I think that was the first leapfrog moment I had. The second leapfrog moment was how to deal with the sixth ingredient that I added to my father's recipe, and that was perseverance. It's never giving up.

ONE GIANT LEAP FROM REJECTION TO TRIUMPH

When I first applied to NASA, I met all of the requirements of being an astronaut. The problem was that more than 12,000 people who also applied met those requirements, so the competition was pretty stiff. I remember the sixth time I got rejected, I crumpled up the rejection letter and was ready to give up. My wife, Adela, found the crumpled letter and confronted me. "I don't know what they have that you don't," she said.

She was talking about the astronauts that were selected. Her words resonated, and I started to closely examine the CVs of the newly selected astronauts. I quickly found that everybody was a pilot and I wasn't. I met the minimum requirements, but I wasn't a pilot. I saw that commonality in them. So, I invested in myself, and I became a pilot. Then I noticed a second thing another year, apart from all being pilots, they were also all scuba divers. I became a basic-certified, advanced-certified, scuba- rescue certified, and a master-certified scuba diver.

It was another leapfrog moment. What I had started doing was getting the attributes, the qualities, and the skills of the people that were being selected so that NASA would see me more like them because, obviously,

those were the traits NASA was looking for. After that sixth rejection, I worked on, not just keeping the minimum requirements and eligibility, but adding to my curriculum, in a way that was consistent with what I thought NASA was seeking. That's how I made that leapfrog to get selected.

THE WORLD IS ONE

Going to space changed me, it changed my perspective of life on our planet. A big moment for me was when I looked through the window pointing straight down towards Earth. I wanted to absorb, seize the moment, and really take it in. When I arrived at the window, we were over North America. I was able to make out Canada, the United States, and Mexico. What struck me was that I couldn't tell where Canada ended and the US began, or where the US ended and Mexico began. That's when it hit me, the realization that we are only one race, 'The Human Race,' and borders are artificial, human-made concepts designed to separate us. It was sad, because from my perspective, looking down, it was evident that we are just one. I would love the opportunity to give all our world leaders that same perspective, that same 'Aha!' moment. If they could see that, I am certain that we wouldn't be having the problems we have in the world.

OUR FRAGILE EARTH

I had a 10-minute break, and it was precisely during a sunrise. We were coming from the dark side of Earth, and the sun was rising on the Earth's horizon. If you wait long enough as the Earth and the sun are revealed in the horizon, the rays of the sun hit the Earth at such an angle that you can see the thickness of our atmosphere. And it's scarily thin. I looked at how fragile it seemed and thought it's the only thing that's keeping us alive on Mother Earth. It was then that I became an instant and impassioned environmentalist. We should be good stewards of our planet so that we can leave the world in an as good or better condition for future generations.

If you look at the Amazon River, the ocean looks beautiful and blue. But then you see at the mouth of the river there is a 500 km brown, semi-circle. That is all the topsoil being dumped into the ocean as a result of deforestation. When you see those effects from space, what mankind is doing to our planet, you can't help but become an ardent environmentalist.

LEGACY IN SPACE

In regard to space exploration, the next logical step is to establish a long-duration lunar base, where instead of going to the station, our astronauts go to the surface of the moon and start developing and testing the technologies that are going to be needed to eventually make our way to Mars. From a scientific perspective, that's what I would like to see, and I think that's in line with what NASA is currently doing.

But my own personal legacy is to be a role model for children, which I feel is a great privilege. I want to help to ensure that education becomes a level playing field and opportunities are open to everyone. For example, through the foundation 'Reach for the Stars', we provide scholarships and programs to support underrepresented groups to thrive in STEM (science, technology, engineering and math) subjects. I present a lot of talks at universities and high schools, and I always think back to that moment when I was ten years old, when a Caucasian astronaut on a black and white TV motivated me to become an astronaut.

There is an adage "You can't be what you can't see." So being able to promote myself as a Hispanic astronaut is something

"When you see what mankind is doing to our planet, you can't help but become an ardent environmentalist."

I take very seriously. These students get to see someone who speaks like them and may come from the same socio-economic background. They see me in person, imagine what kind of motivation that can give them. As a 10-year-old, I was motivated by such a distant role model I saw on a tv screen. Now, to be going into these communities and speaking about the gospel of STEM education, I regard that as an amazing privilege, and a big responsibility. It's an honor.

One of the things that frustrates me most, is that when you're born to this world, it's not a level playing field. I would love to work towards making sure education is available to everyone who needs it because I truly believe education is the great equalizer. There are people out there willing to learn and willing to get educated, but the opportunities for many just aren't there.

I leapfrogged from my front room as a 10-year-old right into space. But the ultimate things that got me there were those little leaps; studying hard, learning, achieving my grades, growing from experience, dealing with rejection, listening intently to my father's advice, and having the resourcefulness to make my dream happen. It isn't always easy to leap in life, but if we are willing to try, we are likely to succeed. It takes many 'Aha!' moments to reach those leaps. When you are lucky enough to springboard into that final leap and reach the highest stars, it is then that you need to look back and remember what and who got you there. To think how you can give back to make life and the world a better place than you found it. I believe it is my duty now to help the potential leapers of today find their lily pads of tomorrow.

> "It isn't always easy to leap in life but if we are willing to try, we are likely to succeed."

To see more on
Jose M Hernandez

LISA BODELL

CEO | Futurist | Global Speaker on Innovation, Simplification and Change
Board Member| Best Selling Author

Just based on her volunteering experience alone, Lisa could be defined as an extraordinary individual. A one-woman movement to end poverty and inequity, she has offered her services in shelters, children's hospitals, soup kitchens, social services, and education. It's an impressive and awe-inspiring list to put on anyone's resume, but what is truly astonishing is that Lisa, who must be one of the busiest people on the planet, still finds the time and motivation to continue with her philanthropic endeavors. There's something fascinating about those at the very top, doing all they can to help those at the bottom.

Her generosity of spirit and true sense of humanity sets Lisa aside from many, but this multifaceted individual has also been the recipient of some notable accolades, including being one of the Top 50 Keynote Speakers in the World, for several years running. Her three buzzwords, 'simplification, innovation, and collaboration' have been featured in her two bestselling publications, *Kill the Company* (2012) and Why Simple Wins (2016). Both books focus on "eliminating barriers to innovation and productivity."

"I think it would be beneficial for the world to be unbusy."

· 27 ·

Lisa is the CEO of FutureThink, a consultancy firm focused on building engaged and highly performing teams. She is recognised as one of the top 50 futurists, a Global Council Member of the World Economic Forum, a contributor to Women@Forbes, Harvard Business Review, and a popular TED talk contributor where she shares her expertise on the "slow pace of fast change" to 100,000 people a year spread over 30 countries.

> "The main issue in the education system is that we are not raising humans, we're raising employees."

As a 'practical Midwesterner' it could be argued that her raison d'etre has its foundation firmly embedded in education, regarding herself foremost as a teacher. She volunteers at The Knowledge Society which helps develop vital skill sets and mindsets, preparing future CEOs and innovators to become world-class thinkers. One could argue the world needs more people like Lisa, who has the energy, foresight, and acumen to drive change on a global scale.

Lisa in her own words...

TIME TO THINK

I am purpose-driven, and education is very important. I do lots of things in schools focusing on innovation, entrepreneurship, and building character in order to help young people reach their full potential. The main issue in the education system is that we are not raising humans, we're raising employees. Here in the US, we are focused on Olympic-level CEOs and athletes, but what we also need to be improving on is how we educate our children. We need to do a better job in teaching them future ready skills like problem solving, curiosity, and collaboration.

What I talk about in the World Economic Forum is how we promote more human-centric behaviors. This is important because successful leaders who will change the world in the future aren't just the ones who know their subject matter, but are the ones who can look between and beyond their business, and get everyone to work together to solve the bigger problems.

We know that companies struggle to find people who can think differently and think bigger, and that's basically down to an education system that doesn't give students time to think. They have time to memorize, to do tests and tasks, but they don't have time to think. And we're not teaching people how to think, or giving them the time and space to think. If schools just got rid of meaningless homework and unnecessary memorization tests, it would leave time for kids to just be curious, to have time to tinker, and be more experimental.

KEEP IT SIMPLE, STUPID

We are in such a fast-paced, changing world that I don't think people have time for theory anymore. Imagine what you could do with the time you spend sitting in meetings and drowning in emails. What if you used that time to do more meaningful work? The front end of innovation is about getting the space to think. People just don't have time to think because they're so busy doing reports, meetings, and emails. The issue is that we're a world that values more, we always want more, whoever has more wins. This desire for 'more' creates busyness, noise, and unnecessary stuff at work and school. We need simplicity, and the movement has to be about making it ok to value less, eliminating unnecessary things to make space for meaningful things.

An approach could be to focus on little things that make a big difference. It's easier to embrace change if we break things down into little parts. Also, instead of focusing on what you are going to do, you need to focus on what you are going to stop doing. That is a real mental shift. In my own life, I stopped a lot of senseless carpools; they just didn't add value. I stopped going to school meetings that weren't going to further the education of my kids, and I started grouping my calls together so I had less context switching.

Schools need someone in charge of killing stupid rules to create space for people to focus better. They should have their own chief innovation officers and chief simplification officers, in order to get rid of all the everyday rubbish to reduce the friction that gets in the way of teachers teaching, and students learning.

> "Leaders who will change the world in the future aren't just the ones who know their subject matter, but are the ones who can look between and beyond their business, and get everyone to work together to solve the bigger problems."

· 29 ·

TIME IS NOT RENEWABLE

We have to challenge how people think, and the pandemic certainly did that to us over the last few years. It has permanently forced us to question not just the way that we think, but the way we work, and bigger than that, the way we live. Companies don't have the same power that they did before the pandemic arose. For example, people are now challenging whether they need to come into the office. Businesses are struggling to figure out how they bring people back to the office. They're fighting against employees who need to see the value in coming back. Businesses are being forced to be more intentional, proactive, and respectful of peoples' time. At the moment, employees have more power than the companies, and they're demanding a more purposeful approach.

My book *Kill the Company* is all about killing stupid rules. Of course, there are smart rules, and they should stay, but there are also a lot of stupid rules, which should undoubtedly go. Killing stupid rules teaches us that there are many things in our sphere of control that we can get rid of. Habits, cultural assumptions, norms, reports, emails, and meetings are all things that get in the way of meaningful work.

For example, killing the amount of meetings you attend and also killing that feeling that you are perhaps not important enough to be attending that meeting. One of the best things we do at my company is tell our clients it's a badge of honor to be uninvited to a meeting because it means your time is too important. It's gotten to the point now where people that are included in the meeting feel like a loser because they think everyone else's time is more important than theirs. To help people better put boundaries on their time, we teach them to respond to requests using YES/IF, which presents trade-offs, as in, 'YES, I'll come to your meeting, IF we can do it at this time.'

We are teaching people how to put boundaries around their time because time is not a renewable resource. If you don't have the power to say no, at least be able to have the power to put some kind of boundaries around it. If you could just get back an hour or two a day, imagine the impact that would have.

We are teaching people how to put boundaries around their time because time is not a renewable resource. If you don't have the power to say no, at least be able to have the power to put some kind of boundaries around it. If you could just get back an hour or two a day, imagine the impact that would have

MAKING SPACE TO LEAPFROG

A leapfrog idea I'm very much into is 'stopping versus starting.' I think it would be beneficial for the world to be unbusy, to stop doing things that are obligations, to stop doing things that aren't meaningful, and to stop being busy, so they can create the space to think and focus on what is really important.

Every morning I carve out 30 minutes of time for myself, and I write whatever I

"If we don't create the space for thinking, we aren't going to be able to have people that can think and LeapFrog."

want. It's like journaling, and that's a cognitive exercise where if you write three pages a day, it doesn't matter what you write about, but you will eventually get to the root cause of what is bothering you or you will get inspired. I try to take as many walking meetings as I can because the neuroscience around just moving 20 minutes a day is phenomenal in terms of what it does, cognitively, to your brain.

THE ART OF PUBLIC SPEAKING

Being on stage is amazing, not only am I learning, I feel it's a magnifier. I'm not just a speaker, I'm a teacher. I've always been fascinated by the things that get the biggest responses, because they are usually the simplest. When I talk about the sphere of control and financial benefits, CEOs care, but when I talk about simple things like killing stupid rules, they're amazed. The simplest things can be a transformation. They actually tell me when they've killed stupid rules. At Accenture, they created a killer stupid rule graveyard, a cemetery with little tombstones where they killed all their rules, and they made it visual.

I use a software package on stage called Mentimeter, to create an interactive connection with the audience. I will ask them a question and their answers come up on the screen, so they participate in the presentation. For example, I will ask them when they do their best thinking. The most common response is in the shower or walking, exercising, driving, those answers are shared on the big screen. The answer that never gets shared on the screen is, the office, no one ever says they do their best thinking in the office. If we don't create the space for thinking, we aren't going to be able to have people that can think and LeapFrog.

BEHAVIOR DRIVEN TECHNOLOGY

As a futurist, I deal in foresight. There are a lot of trends coming up about how we will continue in the future, for instance, we're not going to extract energy, we're going to grow it. But I think a big thing in the future will be behavior, the so-called soft skills, but I call them future-ready skills because these human-centric skills are going to be the key to change, mainly because of technology.

Behavior driven technology like Alexa and smart assistants are resulting in us hiring behavior analysts, or cognitive psychology experts to help programmers. It can either be for good or evil, but nevertheless, there's going to be a lot in the future centering on behavior. For instance, in the future everything will be equipped with a smart assistant. I could have an Alexa or Google in my brainstorming room, and it could calculate, based on the brainstorming session, the probability of the success of all the ideas that were discussed. This seems like a great idea, but on the flip side, it could also act like a surveillance device, monitoring who was in that room, and what they talked about. So, there's a lot of 'cool versus creepy' things that we're going to get into and that we don't know how to handle yet.

"Human-centric skills are going to be the key to change, mainly because of technology."

To see more on
Lisa Bodell

RETHINK ESTABLISHED NORMS

Be ready to challenge accepted ideas and delve into unique approaches to problem-solving. This approach allows us to discover inventive solutions that push past the established norms and pave the way for leapfrogging opportunities. As we journey through the pathways of progress, we often encounter crossroads where the familiar route is not necessarily the most effective or efficient one. Here, the philosophy of leapfrogging takes on a whole new meaning - it's not just about advancing swiftly, but about radically rethinking the established norms.

"Innovation is seeing what everybody has seen and thinking what nobody has thought."

Dr. Albert Szent-Gyorgyi

The capability to question the status quo, to reimagine the familiar, and to seek novel approaches to problem-solving, fosters transformative leaps that can redefine the landscape of progress:

NATIONAL COUNTRY PROGRAMS

Rwanda provides an inspiring example at the national level. Despite having a tragic history, Rwanda leapfrogged development stages by investing heavily in technology and women's empowerment, transforming itself into one of Africa's leading nations in tech and gender equality.

CORPORATES

Take Tesla, for instance. The company completely reimagined the auto industry's accepted norms by creating high-performance electric cars, bypassing the incremental path of hybrid vehicles, and setting new standards in automotive technology.

NEW VENTURES AND STARTUPS

Airbnb challenged the established norms of the hospitality industry. Instead of building more hotels, they developed a platform that turns any house into a potential hotel room, leapfrogging traditional industry practices.

LOCAL COMMUNITY CHANGE

The Barefoot College in rural India challenges traditional education norms by training illiterate women from rural communities to become solar engineers, circumventing traditional schooling methods, and providing practical, life-changing skills.

INDIVIDUAL PERSONAL

Consider the story of Sal Khan, founder of Khan Academy. Instead of adhering to traditional teaching methods, he started creating educational videos for his cousins. Today, Khan Academy provides free, world-class education to anyone, anywhere, leapfrogging conventional education paradigms.

The ability to rethink established norms and challenge the status quo can be a powerful catalyst for leapfrogging. It empowers us to see beyond the obvious, to seek out-of-the-box solutions, and to foster disruptive innovation. As we continue to navigate the complexities of our rapidly evolving world, let's keep questioning, keep reimagining, and keep leapfrogging.

EMILY CHANG

CEO, McCann Worldgroup China | ex-Starbucks, Apple, P&G, IHG | Board Director
best-selling author of The Spare Room

Emily moved with her family to the US when she was a child. As the daughter of Chinese immigrants, she used her experiences to catapult herself into a wide range of leadership positions on a global stage. Her success can be considered partly due to her multicultural upbringing. Having to explain to her non-English speaking mother all about America, and about China to her Western friends, Emily developed "empathetic thinking for mutual understanding." A quality and skill she still leans on today, being able to bridge different disciplines and mindsets.

She has found unprecedented success by "learning to dance to life's rhythms instead of making life march to her own," a philosophy that has taken her down many diverse paths. A compelling business pioneer and distinguished marketer, she has held leadership positions in some of the largest international organizations; Procter & Gamble, Apple, Starbucks, and now as CEO for the advertising giant McCann.

However, it is her social legacy that is perhaps the most

impressive detail in Emily's life. For the past 25 years, she has offered a home to 17 children who were not her own. These were children who needed more than just a spare room, they needed love, care, compassion, and patience, and Emily and her family offered them all of this, and more; these children were offered hope.

During this time, Emily found space to extend her household further. Already living with her husband and young daughter Laini, she found room for 5 dogs, 1 turtle, 1 guinea pig, and, curiously, 129 snails. But she will be most remembered for offering sanctuary, dignity, and a future to children in need; an abused child bride, a baby with a potentially fatal brain condition, and a girl raised in a brothel were just a few of the children lucky enough to have been given a helping hand by Emily's Spare Room.

Splitting her career between the US and China, she is currently based in Shanghai, reading, writing, teaching, and still working, as well as managing to accomplish one new thing each year just to ensure she doesn't forget that feeling of being a novice.

Emily in her own words...

THE MAGIC FORMULA TO LEAPFROG... "PUT THE CONSUMER FIRST."

I think it's imperative to put the consumer first. Get a very clear view of who you serve and understand them better than anyone else. Once you've done that, you then spend your days and nights thinking about how you can delight them in ways that they can't even articulate to you. Then you are ready to start a business.

I believe anyone setting out to build a successful business must not only leverage but also amplify their strengths. In addition to leading with our strengths, we must also identify our weaknesses and mitigate them. And particularly in the startup world, a world of constrained resources, setting aside time to identify our weaknesses requires intentionality. This is critical to sustained

"Get a very clear view on who you serve and understand them better than anybody else. Once you've done that, you then spend your days and nights thinking about how you can delight them in ways that they can't even articulate to you."

success because, while our strengths may compensate for weaknesses in the early days, those vulnerabilities will become more apparent as we grow and scale.

> "We can do more if we're willing to go out on a limb to feel vulnerable, to feel uncertain, to go out into spaces that we've never been in before, and having confidence is a big thing."

THE 'SPARE ROOM' CONCEPT

The idea for my book, *The Spare Room* (2021), came from a TEDx talk I gave called "The Spare Room" in the fabulous Shanghai theater about the experiences I had when offering a room in my home to children in need. TEDx encourages speakers to think about what ideas are worth spreading, so I really felt I needed to think hard for this talk. In fact, I credit the TEDx talk with helping me design the construct of Social Legacy.

I feel very blessed with *The Spare Room* book project. When I started this passion project, I didn't know anything about the publication process. I wasn't sure I was a good enough writer, nor did I know how to find an agent! The whole thing was a sort of experiment, so I pursued the work with curiosity and openness. There were no defined success criteria. Yet, the book was picked up quickly, and published within a year... it even became a bestseller in its category! What I learned was that we often put limitations on ourselves – and if we allow those limitations to define us, we may never step into our biggest possibility. On the other hand, if we're willing to feel uncertain or even vulnerable... to try new things with the clear and present possibility of failure, we may be surprised by what we can do.

At first, I just wanted to tell the stories of these 17 astounding young people and infants who lived in our spare room. I wanted to share what I had learned by watching them transform and what I had learned about the social justice system. However, as the narrative started to develop, it expanded to include other people's stories and formed a model for helping other people identify their own social legacy. This fundamental idea of your 'offer and offense' (the combination of your characteristics, capabilities, and resources, set against the unique opportunity or issue you want to rectify), embedded itself in the theme of the book. If you can find the intersection between those two things, 'offer and offense' you've identified your social legacy, which is your own contribution against something that is calling personally to you.

The concept of 'Spare Room' ended up being a kind of euphemism. What I didn't expect was to have met people who, very literally, opened up their spare rooms, or people who told me about their parents doing the same thing and how they grew up with all kinds of siblings. Through writing the book, I found this unique tribe of people who have lived the same way I have. What an unexpected delight!

FAILURE AS OPPORTUNITY

I have invested half my career in the West and half in the East. And through these two decades, I've discovered so much richness in both parts of the world. There is much that one can learn from the other. Instead of judging or focusing on what we feel the other side doesn't do well, we have the opportunity to flip the lens and consider what does.

For example, Westerners are sometimes perceived as too rigid, traditional, and slow. And yet, they have figured out how to operationalize, and they do this with a high degree of discipline that manages risk profiles quite effectively. On the other hand, the East can sometimes be perceived as a little trigger happy, where they may be seen to 'shoot and then aim.' OK, while they may not have all the rigorous milestones in place before they go to market, they learn and adjust at warp speed! In fact, the Chinese define failure differently. You see, they seek to learn as quickly as possible, and view the idea of launching a flawed product as a great opportunity to learn. Low sales or customer complaints are not perceived as failure. Rather, mistakes that are quickly identified allow for quicker pivots and subsequent success.

SECRETS OF A SUCCESSFUL LEADER

I start each day with 15 minutes of meditation. In this time, I think about the day ahead and what I want to accomplish. Then, I consider what has to happen in order for those goals to be met. You see, many of us have become accustomed to checking emails as soon as we wake up. But what we're essentially doing is starting our day in 'response mode' How much better to approach the day proactively!

I have all kinds of calendar hacks that allow me to balance my time, for example, I don't hold full 1-hour meetings, they have to be, ideally, 45 minutes. We also set many 20-minute meetings, and that may seem really short, but if we know our time limit, we tend to set clear agendas and can accomplish things very quickly. I've gently declined meetings without a clear agenda. That is because we should all be clear on what we seek to get out of a meeting, who should be there, where it should be held, and how long it will take. This enables positive and productive pre-meeting engagement, like ensuring the room is reserved and people can plan commute times. Or adjustments to the invite list, to ensure all the necessary people will be in attendance.

TO RELAX: TIME IS A DISCIPLINE

How do I relax? I operate with operational discipline. Sounds a bit boring, right? Well, if I manage my calendar effectively, I know where my time needs to be spent, and I can prepare for the day accordingly. This ensures I maintain my energy levels, which enables me to be at my best, which ensures that I can best contribute to those around me.

I approach emails with a "one touch" discipline. Once I open an email, I must either respond, delete, or folder it. This always keeps my inbox under one page. Why is this important? Well, if we don't manage our emails, we can easily spend days just chewing through messages! Rather, I like to minimize time in front of the screen and get out on the floor. In my current job, I look after agencies that sit across four floors of a large building in downtown Shanghai. And I don't want to be the kind of leader who is locked away in the office, rarely seen. That's why I build in "walking around time." If we want to be visible, we must intentionally build that time into our calendar and make it a habit. This enables casual engagements across all levels, and frankly, some of the best conversations happen in these in-between moments. Not to mention, walking around is great for my personal wellness. Just taking a five-minute walking break between meetings helps maintain equilibrium and health.

TO CHANGE THE WORLD: CONTRIBUTE MORE THAN WE CONSUME

I love this Balinese proverb I once read: "One hundred years, all new people." That puts it into perspective, doesn't it! Well, I'm at the halfway mark now, so I'm committed to not wasting a moment of this one precious life.

I lead a lot of younger people in the creative world, and I can see some of them struggling with direction. Yet, these amazing humans are filled with potential! They're so smart and equipped with much more than I feel I was when I was their age. Yet, they also live with more stress. If they aren't intentionally

"Rich conversations happen in the casual, and it's the job as a leader to create that casual space."

seeking equilibrium and maintaining wellness, they can quickly feel overwhelmed and want to just give up. The Chinese have a phrase for this, "tang ping," or "lying flat." What a waste of potential! As a leader, I feel my job (and my greatest privilege) is to help young people realize and unleash their potential!

> "Mistakes quickly identified allow for quicker pivots and subsequent success."

To see more on
Emily Chang

ANTHONY THOMSON

Chairman, Zip Co UK
iNED Wio Bank Abu Dhabi

Considered a financial marketing guru, Anthony Thomson is the founder and former chairman of three banks on two continents. In 2010 he launched Metro Bank, the UK's first high street bank in 150 years. A new kind of bank which broke away from tradition, offering customers exceptional service and convenience. Imagine a bank open 7 days a week, 361 days of the year, a bank where your furry best friend can accompany you, welcomed with a smile and a biscuit, a bank where the customer truly comes first.

A consummate business builder, Anthony believes deeply that profit is a result of giving customers a better product, service, or experience. If you do that, and you manage your business well, it will be profitable. It's this unequivocal mindset that's at the heart of his core values. He left school with few qualifications and learned his trade through working with others. It is clear that ambition, intelligence, and passion have been integral to Anthony's many successes. A marketer at heart, fintech pioneer, and atypical banking executive, he is the founder of Metro Bank and atom bank in the UK, Bank 86 400 in Australia and he currently sits on boards in the UK, the middle east and Australia.

> "I often get asked for the secret of my success and I always say that there is no secret - Every morning I get out of bed and go to work. That's it."

Anthony has lectured as a visiting professor at various universities and is also requested to speak at events sharing his expertise on business agility and raising capital. He's a published author and has several roles as an advisor and non-executive director. For a young man leaving school at 17, he has reached the pinnacle of a remarkable career but still remembers his humble beginnings. Recounting life as a "15-year-old with no money," he used to walk three miles just to look at a Gibson Les Paul guitar and dreamed that one day he would own one. Today he feels fortunate enough to own many guitars. His other passions include racing cars and collecting fine wine.

Anthony's Reflections

MY THOUGHTS ON TRUST

Technology is making a huge difference in our lives, but some of the most innovative things we have seen happen over the last 20 years have been culturally driven, or through transformations of thinking rather than innovations of technology.

In 2010, when I started my first bank, the key shift was recognizing that what really mattered to customers was the concept of value. The existing banks all thought that the only thing that mattered to the customers was price. Generally, banks would offer what looked like the best rates for savings and the lowest rates for loans, but of course, they had this 'bait-and-switch' technique where they would entice customers in on a deal which at first appeared to be a low rate and very quickly worked it up.

It became very clear to me that value was most important and value was about much more than price, it was also about service, convenience, and trust. I learned that trust matters to customers - can I trust this person or company that I am dealing with?

There was a real dilemma in the banking sector at the time. Consumer groups found that customers simply did not trust banks, whilst the banks were coming up with a massive amount of research that said their customers did trust them. They couldn't both be, right? But it turns out they were.

> "All these little 'value points' really mattered to people. We demonstrated how value is not simply about price, it is also about convenience and service."

Psychology tells us that there are two types of trust - cognitive trust and associated trust. Cognitive trust is about competence. For example, do I trust that when I put my card into the ATM of a big bank, money will come out? Yes, of course I do. Do I trust that if my salary goes into the big bank on the last day of the month, it will still be there on the first day of the following month? Yes, I do. Do I trust that if I set up a regular payment for my rent or my mortgage, the big bank will pay it? Yes.

People trust banks cognitively. They trust them to be competent. Associated trust is slightly different. For example, do I trust that the big bank has my best interests at heart? Very often, the answer is no. The leapfrogging opportunity for me was not through technological innovation, it was simply recognizing an opportunity to show customers that my bank genuinely did have their best interests at heart, a better product, a better service, and a better customer experience.

That is why, when I started Metro Bank in 2010, we opened seven days a week to enable people to bank on weekends, not just on weekdays when they were typically at work. We also opened from eight in the morning to late at night so people could bank before and after work. We welcomed customers' dogs into our branches, providing water and biscuits. Customers innately understood that if we were committed to looking after their dogs, we'd be committed to looking after their banking needs too! All these little 'value points' mattered to people. We demonstrated how value is not simply about price, it is also about convenience and service.

MOBILE BANKING

The great dilemma of banking used to be a trade-off between offering people either cheap banking services or good banking services. There is a cost implication for each option, and, traditionally, the banks attempted to balance one against the other so you could go to a high street bank that didn't really look after you but was cheap, or you could go to one of the private banks, who looked after you incredibly well but charged a great deal of money for the privilege.

"People can have brilliant ideas wherever they are in this world, they are not restricted to rich or poor, black or white, or any particular ethnic minorities - everybody has the ability and the capacity to have great ideas."

Mobile banking has changed everything because it is both very efficient and cost-effective, which, perhaps surprisingly, comes up with the highest customer satisfaction scores. I say surprisingly because people are saying that by serving themselves, they are getting the best service. That is the new reality because customers want to bank when, where, and how it suits them. And they want to do it in the simplest way; they just want to get it done. Nobody has ever woken up in the morning and said: "Oh, great, I can do some banking today!"

Mobile banking apps enable customers to do exactly what they want, when they want, and usually without too much fuss. Customers can do their banking wherever they are in the world and quickly move on to the more important things in their lives. Mobile banking was a Leapfrog moment for the industry and has been transformational.

FINANCIAL INCLUSION

One of the problems with financial inclusion One of the problems with financial inclusion from a bank's perspective was that it simply cost too much money to serve certain people. Digitization and the use of mobile banking have now become so ubiquitous that they have driven down the cost of serving customers, meaning that those who were previously excluded from banking and similar services can access them.

As we talk about financial inclusion, a far bigger problem today is financial literacy and how, in a highly emotive way, it can seriously affect people's lives. For five years, I chaired The National Skills Academy for Financial Services, where I was incredibly proud of the work we did with abused spouses in the city of Liverpool.

Occasionally the abuse was towards men, but mostly the abuse was directed at women. What we discovered was that the abused partner stayed with their abuser for financial reasons. Through education, we were able to help abused people understand that they had financial options outside of their partners.

I am also very pleased to be involved with the Financial Times' Financial Literacy Inclusion Campaign, which is about helping disadvantaged people understand more about money. I have seen some horrific facts concerning credit cards, including research conducted amongst young people who actually thought that the higher the interest rate, the better the outcome for them. This is awful, and highlights just one of the many reasons we need more financial education for disadvantaged people. I think that technology helps, but effective change requires more human intervention.

LEAPFROGGING WITH WILL.I.AM

Will and I are from very different backgrounds. He's from East LA, and I am from North East England, but we discovered that we had many similarities. Having both grown up in very poor environments, we share a passion for helping underprivileged people. He told me that, generally, the only ways somebody could get out of his community were by joining a gang, dealing drugs, or becoming an athlete or musician.

Will set up his i.am Angel Foundation, which helps disadvantaged people in LA with STEM (Science, Technology, Engineering, Maths) subjects. He is an incredibly creative guy, developing an idea for a collaborative software tool that enables entrepreneurs, or those he calls 'urban creatives,' to compete equally with bigger businesses. It is still very early on in the journey, but it is exhilarating to see it grow. Will is always great fun to work with, and it's been wonderful to see people who were otherwise unable to compete in the gig economy and, perhaps, struggling having the tools to help them succeed.

GEOGRAPHY IS NO DISCRIMINATOR

One thing I have learned while traveling and working around the world, is that nobody has a monopoly on good ideas, we see great ideas come from everywhere. Perhaps the most exciting developments I've seen have come out of Africa. There have been fantastic innovations in Russia and Ukraine too, which proves that geography is no discriminator. People can have brilliant ideas wherever they are in the world, they are not restricted to rich or poor, black or white, or any particular ethnic minority. Everybody has the ability and the capacity to have great ideas. I think the responsibility is upon people like us to help them develop those ideas and to leapfrog.

HOW TO CHANGE THE WORLD

For me, it is a cultural thing, and it's about helping young people develop a mindset to realize there are no limitations to their thinking, their abilities, or the work they are doing. When I was young, the world seemed like a big and challenging place. Therefore, I want to help young people understand that if they have an idea, if they have a vision, they should go for it and that, fortunately, there are people around the world who will help them to deliver that idea.

I like to remind people about possibilities with this question: How do you eat an elephant? You eat it one hamburger at a time. However big the problem is, you start with one little bit and solve that, then move on to the next little bit, and so on. Then

"Nobody has a monopoly on good ideas, we see great ideas come from everywhere."

you enroll friends and family who can help, and you get wise counsel from people who have seen the problem before and enlist their help to solve the problem. It doesn't matter how big a problem is, start by biting off the first piece.

THE SECRET TO SUCCESS

I often get asked for the secret of my success, and I always say that there is no secret - every morning I get out of bed and go to work, that's it.

Launching a bank is very expensive. You cannot open a bank with a few thousand dollars and then put more money in as it grows, you have to build a 'whole bank' for the first customer from day one; for Metro Bank, that required raising $100 million.

In the UK, trying to raise that amount in 2008, everybody thought I was crazy, so I went to America, where they were more open to the concept of new banks. We were working six to eight road shows a day, five days a week, for three weeks, up and down the East Coast, from Baltimore to Philadelphia to New York, to Connecticut, to Boston, back and forwards and back again - it was an incredibly grueling experience, but at the end of three weeks, we had firm commitments for $116 million.

I flew back to the UK, and for the first and only time ever, I got a free upgrade from British Airways! They put me in business class, and I was sitting there having a glass of champagne thinking 'wow, we've done it, this is real, this is going to happen.' I arrived home the next morning and shared the great news with my wife. Then, on Monday 8th September 2008, Lehman Brothers went bust, and from a commitment of $116 million, $65 million disappeared that first week. Within three weeks, it had all gone.

There was the obvious temptation to simply give up, to think that we had given it a go and done our best, that circumstances were way beyond our control. I did not do that. Instead, I got out of bed the very next day, went back to the office, and just kept going. We had a tough eight months bootstrapping ourselves, but then the market started to improve, and we received calls from people asking if we were still planning to launch. We re-started the road shows and were able to raise the capital. I got up, got out of bed, and I went to work. That is what made the difference.

**To see more on
Anthony Thomson**

SPOT LEAPFROGGING OPPORTUNITIES

Seek out areas that are ripe for leapfrogging. By bypassing some steps, we can achieve quicker progress and substantial benefits, carving new pathways to reach our goals more effectively. In the ever-evolving landscape of progress, opportunities for leapfrogging are often hidden in plain sight. Harnessing these chances requires a keen sense of observation and the foresight to spot areas ready for leapfrogging.

> *"Opportunities don't happen.*
> *You create them."*
>
> *Chris Grosser*

By sidestepping some traditional steps, we can make rapid strides and gain significant benefits, forging fresh routes to reach our objectives more efficiently.

NATIONAL COUNTRY PROGRAMS

Estonia presents an excellent national example. Recognizing the transformative power of digitization, the country skipped intermediate stages and transitioned directly to a digital society, becoming one of the most advanced digital nations in the world.

Google, for instance, saw the opportunity to leapfrog existing search engines by developing an algorithm based on the relevance of web pages, significantly improving the search experience for users worldwide.

NEW VENTURES AND STARTUPS

Consider Spotify. Instead of following the established model of owning music, they leapfrogged to a subscription-based streaming service, revolutionizing the way we consume music.

LOCAL COMMUNITY CHANGE

In Bangladesh, Grameen Bank spotted an opportunity to leapfrog traditional banking structures. They provided microloans to those who lack collateral, transforming the economic landscape of rural communities.

INDIVIDUAL PERSONAL

Take the case of Richard Branson. Diagnosed with dyslexia, he chose to leapfrog traditional employment and set up his own business. His Virgin Group is now a global brand in multiple industries, showing how personal challenges can create leapfrogging opportunities.

Spotting opportunities for leapfrogging involves recognizing areas where rapid progress and significant benefits can be made by skipping traditional steps. As we navigate our ever-changing world, let's remember to keep our eyes open for such opportunities, using them to innovate, leap, and progress.

KYLE KANE

Award-Winning Solver of Problems; Brand Strategist; Philanthropist & TEDx Speaker

Kyle Kane is one of those people that, once met, you never forget. He brings an infectious energy that infuses every area of his life. His roots were in music but, now he is currently the Chief Marketing Officer of Nobody Studios. And it's a role he is passionate about, having always described himself as playing many 'human' roles.

He has worked closely and successfully with many household names such as Kylie Jenner, Katy Perry, Samsung, and Universal Music Group and openly dedicates his life to the idea of providing value to all who work with him. His 'value added' concept is demonstrated with his brand-building company, 180 South which was ranked 13th in the Top 500 list of Fastest Growing Companies in America and landed on the 24th rank for Global Marketing and Advertising.

Although he believes there should be no difference between work and life, Kyle enjoys watching sports of fierce competitive battle for the top spot. Fortunately, this thirst for athletic warfare doesn't roll over into his work strategies, where he takes a more collaborative approach and, as such is recognized as a philanthropist, and entrepreneur. An approachable, inspirational leader with ideas that not only span the globe but seeks to improve it.

Kyle in his own words...

There is no dichotomy to work and life. My passions are linked, I am an artist, and that is why I became involved as a 'nobody' at Nobody Studios. I'm a builder of builders and simply have to continue to build. Not a moment is wasted. I still write songs for some of your favorite pop stars and create marketing strategies for some of your favorite brands. I find the same creative outlet in the studio that I experience in the boardroom."

"I truly believe that in a 'people first' mentality, there is no one idea, company, or transaction, which is worth more than the people creating it."

LINKING BRANDS TO ARTISTS - UNDERSTANDING THE VALUE OF LIVE EVENTS.

Supporting Shakira on tour gave me the opportunity to experience people with English as a second language singing my song lyrics in vast arenas. It was a joy to hear and simply another area of my work/fun 'non-dichotomy' life, as was working with some of the biggest names in the creative world and start-up industry. I see no separation between work and personal life and having found this perfect balance of happiness in every aspect of what I do, I believe that I have ultimately enriched my soul and fueled my drive by identifying value and bringing success to those individuals with great passion. I have done this through creative expression and personal beliefs which have extended into every aspect of my existence.

Connected to artists and media alike, and also as a songwriter and recording artist, I am fortunate to be known throughout the music industry and celebrity realm as highly creative and intuitive. As the CEO of the 'Wanna Be Self Group', I have been responsible for crafting the tastes and tones of major brand partnerships including Katy Perry, Samsung, Rihanna, Vita Coco, and the Kylie Jenner and Daniel Wellington project. I truly believe that in a 'people first' mentality, there is no one idea, company, or transaction which is worth more than the people creating it.

We were 'leapfrogging' for others by arranging events, logos, and marketing, and it became apparent that we also needed to fully invest in what we had created, so we decided to become producers of the events, and we raised $15m to make this transition possible just before the covid lockdowns hit! No need to expand further on that! However, through the resilience of entrepreneurial spirit, we subsequently recovered much of that funding. That was also the time I met the Nobody Studios team. It's probably the last organization I will ever need to be with, as our shared vision and paradigm shift is something I will enjoy making work, but it will take energy, focus, and time.

THERE IS MUCH MORE TO LIFE THAN LABELS. THERE IS A LEAP WE CAN ALL TAKE.

Jeff Bezos once stated that *"we have two choices; to either choose a life of comfort and ease, or a life of service and adventure. When you reach 80 and look back, which of those choices do you think you will be most happy with?"*

"I think we must choose a life of adventure. Sometimes it is risky, sometimes it hurts, sometimes you bleed and you scrape, but that is the path I believe we are here for. "

I think we must choose a life of adventure. Sometimes it is risky, sometimes it hurts, sometimes you bleed, and you scrape, but that is the path I believe we are here for.

That was the Leapfrog for me, the awareness that I am not this body, or the experiences that I am going through, and that I have more to give to the world than just the 24 hours in a day. Recognizing the journey of the soul, that I am residing in this meat-covered skeleton floating on a rock through space, and there's really nothing to be scared of, allows me to experience and express the unique qualities of the soul. The gifts I've been given, and my true happiness, comes from my application of those and being able to find the value that I can contribute. I am not the body, not the feelings or the emotions that pass through me. I'm not the anxiety or the depression or the bipolar I was diagnosed with. Those are just the labels, and through a separation of yourself from those things, you can become lovingly detached.

You have two choices, the first is that you can remain with the accepted labels, the second is to choose to build scar tissue and not to let this stuff impact you. I chose not to be labeled; I chose to make a conscious effort to stay open.

TIME TRAVEL: ART AND SCIENCE GO HAND IN HAND

I work in six time zones, in some cases for 22 hours a day, and I am now too old to spend even one moment on something that I'm not passionate about. My passion for creation and innovation is my ability to build businesses. I apply that same thinking, and that same level of creativity, to the messaging that is going to impact buying power and spending habits, and to observe what is perhaps superficial versus what is really required to fill a need in the community.

I believe art and science go hand in hand, and whether you are launching a song, a film, or a new company, it is the art of understanding, the focused thinking that helps key messaging reach its intended audience so that you can introduce someone to a new product, service, or idea, that might change the world. Without that focus, it is extremely tough to cut through the noise in the digital jungle. As a marketer and a human, it is my job to help authentic brands cut through the noise to be noticed and heard.

INNOVATION AND THE FUTURE ARE HERE AND NOW

I have been asked why we use the term 'rebel' in our business description, and I think in this context, specifically, when we say 'rebel', it is much like Leapfrog. It is about resisting traditions and staying open to new ways of thinking.

In my understanding, leapfrogging refers to the exploration of alternative patterns. And that is exactly what we are doing. At Nobody Studios, we are independently minded and want our lives, actions, and investments to be a true expression of our values. Those values are also attracting like-minded people to our journey. Ultimately, they will join us in driving innovation and leaping with us into the future.

For me, the terms 'Rebel' and 'Leapfrogging' represent an opportunity to think outside of the box. We can challenge new and existing ideas and it gives us the flexibility to pioneer and explore the unique. For example, as a team, we have been recently working on an 'explainer' video concept for a web launch. It talks about the mind being similar to a mountain covered with snow and that throughout our lives, we are all often, or consistently going down the same tracks, the same thought patterns. The analogy is that we are building familiar grooves in the mountain snow. The explainer video suggests an expansion of neuroplasticity, an ability to throw a fresh layer of snow on those old tracks, covering them up, and therefore creating new ways around the mountain to solve an issue or problem.

The connection between the left and right brain, that fluidity, those are the possibilities we want to embrace, they have the potential to leapfrog old thinking. When we use terms like 'Rebel' or 'Leapfrogging' as ideas, we are playing into a powerful notion. They are a way to forget about the tracks and grooves of the past and lay fresh 'virgin' snow to tread on and be excited about. Let us all look at the future from a new angle and enjoy it together.

SUPERPOWER TO LEAPFROG

The concept of empathy should be regarded as a superpower. If you have the ability to see your offerings from all perspectives, it's then possible to create an ecosystem around a particular product, idea, or company creation. Some people who are contributing to your journey know the practical value of what you're creating, and by not losing sight of that practical application, by standing in others' shoes, we are sure to make something that is of use, something that is relevant.

Ultimately, that's the idea of rebel and leapfrog to me. Those are the words that take us in a progressive direction. They both have the potential to bring our aspirations and progressive leaps forward, into a life and future of worth.

GROWTH IS MULTIPLE LEAPFROGS

I don't think that I can point to any one leapfrog moment that was responsible for our growth. I think it has been more like 50, or 100 things, each of them contributing a small percentage which then adds up to massive change.

This is especially true in the venture space where we can specifically talk to the needs of the community that have been annexed, where we have this proprietary company creation model that gets people excited. We can evaluate and validate ideas very quickly. For the ones that pass the test, we can scale, and for the ones that don't, we can let go. We have the ability to control the narrative in that way. Each one of those percentage incremental advancements in the process becomes its own leapfrog.

LEAPFROGGING THE COMPETITION: FRUGAL, CREATIVE AND AGGRESSIVE

I think our progressive venture capital model is ground-breaking. It is this new approach that is going to leapfrog the next 100 companies which are going to change the world. I don't think that the company creation process in the entrepreneur community is currently ready to handle what we are going to need in a fast-moving world. Nobody Studios is a team of rockstar entrepreneurs who leave their egos at the door to shred the traditional VC model and solve the world's problems one company at a time. Nobody Studios' registered trademark stands for, frugal, creative, and aggressive. The idea of this model is where all the work happens because we are deliberately 'irrationally' global and sourcing wonderful ideas from solutions all around the world. We are completely transparent, allowing everyone we engage with to see each step of the process, and we are crowd-infused. That means that every single idea graduates with an army of influencers ready to bring it to the market.

> "The concept of empathy should be regarded as a superpower."

ARE WE READY TO LEAPFROG OUR WAY INTO THE FUTURE?

The culture and development of our industry are changing, and I believe it's all going to happen much quicker than we expect. Prepare for that. Our chief 'nobody', Mark McNally, always talks about the idea of demystifying what it takes to go big. That is part of our greater challenge, because if these changes happen sooner than we think, and our minds are not prepared, then we are in for a rude awakening.

This problem is industry-specific, it is a global problem, one that we can only solve through diversity in thinking. That is why we are embracing the core values of crowd-infused, and people first, because we do need to tap into that whole collective to be able to solve these problems.

WE CAN ONLY CONTROL OURSELVES

The world in general, and the countries within it have unique needs and vastly different 'lily pads' from which to leapfrog. Probably the hardest lesson I have learned is that no matter how much we want to think we can help others to leapfrog, the truth is that we can only control ourselves. All of our leapfrogs are within ourselves. I practice integrity, work harder than anyone I know across multiple time zones and show up consistently for those people that I love. I try my utmost to contribute value every day and leave this world better than I found it. This is easy to say, but much harder to do. To wake up every day and do that consistently is important to me. I know that the work I do ultimately becomes the legacy that I leave. That is all I can control, and that is what I am focused on.

INVEST IN YOURSELF, AND IN YOUR MIND, TO INVEST IN OTHERS

I meditate, do a lot of breathwork, and practice some Qigong. When I was younger, I was an extrovert and that has largely been sacrificed. My new fun is in my mind, I escape by exploring myself through destinations and traveling to places that I can only imagine. Some people hunt, fish, play golf, or indulge in 'recreational' pursuits, and I feel that there is nothing wrong with any of those things. But for me, the real joy is in spending time with myself. I normally have two or three meetings every hour, therefore, any moment that I can get with silence and peace, and be inwardly reflective, is worth more to me now than attending the best music festival on the planet.

My leapfrog message to the world of entrepreneurs and all of humanity is to learn to look after yourself, invest in you:

Create a better world for yourself, by doing what you love. Life is too short not to do what you love all the time.

Listen to your body, it knows what's good for you, and most importantly, what is not.

Drink half of your body weight in ounces of water every day.

Get real rest, most important problems are solved while you're sleeping.

Don't overthink things. Trust your gut, rely on it, it is truly your intelligence.

THE METAPHOR

Leapfrog is such a cool metaphor because if there is magic in the world, it is surely found under those lily pads in the water, just as it's found in us. And if there's magic in the body, it is found through the breath, and our ability to connect.

Believe in you. You have the power to create change for yourself and the world.

Use that energy to leapfrog into your future.

> **"Create a better world for yourself, by doing what you love."**

To see more on
Kyle Kane

JOE FOSTER

Founder of Reebok

In 1958 Joe Foster, with his brother Jeff, founded Reebok. The name in itself was a difficult decision for the pair, who had their hearts set on Mercury, evoking a sense of movement and fluidity. Unfortunately, another shoe company had got there first, and the brothers were back to the drawing board, in Joe's living room. With a bottle of beer in one hand and a dictionary in the other, they found the perfect name - Reebok - an antelope known for being 'light, fast and agile,' a promising name for a sports shoe company.

Coming from a long line of shoemakers, Joe's entrepreneurial journey resulted in the iconic brand becoming a legacy, defining a generation and changing the face of sports retailing forever. At one point, around 60% of the USA's population owned a pair of Reeboks. The shoes were seen on red carpet events, Sigourney Weaver wore a pair in the film Aliens, and perhaps more importantly, athletes wearing the shoes were setting world records and winning Olympic, Commonwealth, and European medals.

It's been a rollercoaster life with many ups and downs, tragedies, and triumphs, all documented in his autobiography 'Shoemaker.' He is a shining example of how to live a life of purpose, take a wealth of life experience and leapfrog a new generation. With the enthusiasm and drive of a man half his age, Joe continues to speak to audiences around the world recounting his success and celebrating his One Golden Nugget - Just Keep Going!

Joe shares his thoughts on...

LEAPFROGGING

"In life you need a lot of patience and a lot of effort. You also need a good healthy chunk of luck."

In business, you need a lot of patience and a lot of effort. You also need a healthy chunk of good luck. It can take a while, but when the opportunity does arrive, you need to have the awareness to both notice it and take advantage of it. By the late 1970s, we had built Reebok into a $4m company in the UK, but my dream was always to take the American market with 330 million people with disposable incomes. The UK simply wasn't big enough for my aspirations.

Our first trip to the States was in 1968, and we endured 11 years of perseverance, disappointments, and knockbacks. However, when Runners' World developed a star rating system, things started to change dramatically for the company. With six failed attempts behind us, we finally got a distribution foothold in the US market thanks to three of our running shoes landing five-star reviews in the magazine. Up until 1979, it had always nominated Nike as the number one shoe in the US. Yet Reebok knew how to make a 5-star shoe, it was as simple as that.

Even though we had a stellar product, we were never big enough to truly compete with the likes of Adidas and Nike in the market. It was only in the early 80's, when aerobics began to take off, that we finally found some 'white space'. With aerobics, we had found our niche and it was then that Reebok transformed from a $9 million business, to a $1 billion business in just over five years. By the late 1980s, Reebok had overtaken Adidas and Nike to become the number-one brand in sports shoes in the USA.

LEAPFROGGING NIKE

Our competitors' brands were seen as very masculine, sweaty, heavy sports brands. Reebok was seen as a shoe for women. At that time, women's fashion changed more quickly than its male equivalent, and there was always demand for the next shoe, the next colorway, and the next technical development.

Our biggest problem was how we could keep up with demand and continue to grow at speed. Again, we were lucky. Nike was the biggest brand at that time, but they had to pull out of many factories in South Korea exactly when we needed these facilities. Did we use that as a leapfrog? Of course we did. Our mindset was very much that we had to take this gift to win.

Manufacturing in the UK had become too expensive, and suddenly this opportunity arose in South Korea where, not only did they have the space and the machinery, but crucially they had the expertise and willingness to take us on.

In business, you must have the awareness to spot and take an opportunity. And, critically, you also need tenacity, determination, and a winning mentality to leapfrog a competitor. It was a defining moment.

"With aerobics, we had found our niche and it was then that Reebok transformed from a $9 million business, to a $1 billion business in just over five years."

FROM INFLUENCING TO LEAPFROGGING

My grandfather influenced key people. Back then, it was just about pure performance. His influence was founded on athletes winning races and setting records. Over the years, since those early 'influencer' days, the market has changed and is now vastly more to do with street, fashion, and a focus on volume sales.

The volumes achieved by focusing on performance were important but not comparable to what we expect today. Back then, my grandfather would simply give his JW Foster products to athletes who were winning races. They, in turn, influenced the teams and the club runners who wished to emulate these top athletes by wearing JW Foster shoes. The results spoke for themselves and proved that 'technologically advanced' shoes would help them win races.

When my brother Jeff and I created Reebok, my grandfather's strategy was a plan we continued. We gave shoes to lead athletes like Ron Hill, and because he did well when wearing our crafted products, he influenced others to follow.

When we finally entered the American market, after an eleven-year challenge, we discovered aerobics, and Reebok took off in a different way. Aerobics was a new phenomenon in Los Angeles. It was a glamorous form of exercise, and Jane Fonda wore a pair of Reeboks in her exercise videos. Women loved them and wore them in the street, the first 'street shoe' if you like, and Reebok caught on within the aerobics craze, which was mainly driven by women.

In Hollywood, because Jane Fonda had chosen to wear Reebok, and that was a huge influence on other 'A-List' celebrities who started to wear our new 'soft and female' driven shoes. Cybill Shepherd and her friends were into Reeboks, and it took off like a rocket. That was a leapfrog moment, an incredible shift. I feel, in many ways, that was the beginning of the 'influencing culture' we see today. We took our product from a purely performance item onto the street and into a fashion statement.

'SERIOUS' LEADERSHIP

I firmly believe you must get the right people in a company to develop a winning culture. People regularly ask me the three most important things in growing a company and I tell them:

First, it must be fun...
Secondly, you have got to have more fun!
Thirdly, it must be absolute fun, because if you are not enjoying the journey, you can't do it. You must have moments of joy to maintain that intense desire to carry on.

Running a company takes a considerable amount of your time, so it must be something that you enjoy – I don't mean every day, there are always challenges, but overall, you must be having a great time. This way, new people will want to join your company because they can see the passion, the successes, and the joy that makes the harder moments worthwhile.

Of course, it is a prerequisite that you have a great product, one that you understand inside and out, but if you can enjoy the long hard hours and successes together, you forget the failures!

I had a lot of failures. I failed six times to procure a distributor for Reebok in the United States. There was one particular person, a man I had hoped to work with, who I chased for four years without success. Like often happens, there were many failures, but at the same time, I was learning every day. Six years of struggle equals a lot of learning.

Each time we failed, I kept thinking of what we had done wrong and how we could put it right next time. I learned that what I needed, fundamentally, was somebody who was as hungry and needed to succeed as much as Reebok. Eventually, we found the right distributor, one with the right mindset, and the rest, as they say, is history.

IDEAS CHANGE THE WORLD

The biggest change that Reebok made to the global market, certainly as far as sports footwear is concerned, was to shift to the use of soft leather.

Before this, 'everyday shoes,' especially the better quality ones, were made of stiff leather which required 'breaking in,' which meant they needed to be worn over time to feel nice. Without this process, quality footwear could give you problems with blisters and could be quite painful until, eventually, they would become comfortable and last for many years.

Sports shoes were similar, though not exactly like quality formal shoes, they still needed to be worn in. A shoe is a three-dimensional object. When you make a shoe on a wooden mold, or last as it is called, and then remove the shoe, it has to hold its shape. Leather is fairly firm, but it has two other important complementary qualities, plasticity and elasticity, and these are affected by treating and stretching it in various ways.

We wanted to use a leather that was so soft that it was right at the margin of its viability. In other words, we wanted it so fine that any more stretching would cause it to break. Reebok was a woman's shoe; therefore, instant comfort was essential.

We needed a material that was super comfortable on the feet, but still practical. As a material, glove leather was far too thin, so we worked with the tanneries to create a leather that was still soft, but stronger and able to hold its shape better. It was an industry game-changer. Now, when you look on the street, most footwear is sports-driven, and it's soft, so you don't have to break it in. This was, and continues to be, the big change, the leapfrog Reebok introduced.

Today there are many innovations in the world that I embrace, including the ability to conduct business at a distance and the ability to connect in a way that was impossible when I built Reebok. I often imagine what I could achieve now if starting to build again!

"Six years of failure equals a lot of learning."

To see more on
Joe Foster

· 69 ·

NURTURE A CULTURE OF INNOVATION

Foster a culture that values creativity, trial and error, and ongoing innovation. Such an environment encourages people and organizations to think differently and apply novel innovations to make leapfrog leaps forward. In the orchestra of progress, innovation is the maestro. It holds the baton of creativity, inspires the symphony of trial and error, and crafts a masterful score that transforms mere notes into melodious leapfrog leaps. Cultivating this culture of innovation is akin to nurturing a garden where ideas can bloom and thrive.

> *"Innovation distinguishes between a leader and a follower."*
>
> *Steve Jobs*

A culture that cherishes creativity, embraces failure as a learning curve, and perpetually seeks innovation, encourages people and organizations to think divergently and apply groundbreaking innovations to surge forward.

NATIONAL COUNTRY PROGRAMS

Singapore's Smart Nation initiative is an outstanding example of promoting innovation on a national level. With a vision to drive economic growth and improve lives, the initiative has spurred a culture of innovation across sectors, from technology and healthcare to transportation.

CORPORATES

Take, for instance, Amazon. They have a deep-seated culture of innovation, experimenting with everything from delivery drones to cashier-less stores, always seeking to redefine the customer experience.

NEW VENTURES AND STARTUPS

SpaceX is another example. They've instilled an innovation culture, aiming to redefine space travel and make multi-planetary life a reality, leapfrogging over conventional aerospace constraints.

LOCAL COMMUNITY CHANGE

In the rural regions of Africa, Ushahidi has developed an innovative crowdsourcing tool to report violence, turning local communities into powerful data sources and leapfrogging traditional information barriers.

INDIVIDUAL PERSONAL

Elon Musk embodies this principle at a personal level. His innovative approach to electric vehicles with Tesla, and his ambitious space exploration projects with SpaceX, demonstrate how nurturing an innovation culture can drive monumental leaps forward.

Nurturing a culture of innovation is crucial in our leapfrogging journey. It calls for embracing creativity, learning from failures, and continuously pursuing innovation. As we tread the path of progress, let's remember that our greatest leaps forward often come from thinking differently and daring to innovate.

EZECHI BRITTON MBE

Tech Founder, Early Stage Investor & NED

Ezechi Britton MBE has made his way in life with determination, focus and strength. Named MBE in the 2022 Queen's Honors List for services to diversity in young people, he co-founded Code Untapped, a social enterprise set up to train the next generation of underrepresented technologists.

He is a founding member, principal investor, and Chief Technology Officer for Impact X Capital, a venture capital company supporting underrepresented entrepreneurs across Europe and Afro-Caribbean diaspora. In April 2023, Ezechi will start a new role as the first CEO of CFIT the UK's Centre for Finance, Innovation and Technology an industry body backed by HM Treasury and the City of London Corporation with a mandate to unblock barriers to growth for financial technology companies and to lead the world in financial innovation.

Not only has Ezechi made an impact throughout his career, but he is also amazing at martial arts, being a qualified karate instructor, Tai boxer, and gym enthusiast. He's also a huge fan

> "I launched a Fintech start-up in 2014, called Neyber. The company raised over £200m and we lent out over £170m to UK-based employees."

of extreme sports, he's a qualified snowboarding instructor and loves climbing. An avid gamer and sports enthusiast, it's fortunate Ezechi still finds time to make his mark by helping to create a better world.

Ezechi made an extraordinary leapfrog in life when he jumped from being an investment banking technologist at Lehman Brothers and Credit Suisse, to co-founding businesses with a social purpose, either supporting underrepresented groups to progress in tech, providing financial wellbeing packages to employees, or investing money to help end homelessness. Choosing to work with the disadvantaged to make the world a better place, he embraces non-traditional solutions if it means furthering the cause.

He brings inspiration, as well as positive encouragement, and drive to everything he does, and most importantly he does it with integrity.

Ezechi in his own words...

LEAPFROGGING FROM LEWISHAM TO SWITZERLAND

When people hear me, they listen to someone that is well-spoken, and people automatically assume a certain level of education and background. The reality is that I grew up in Lewisham, South East London, and I went to a very terrible, comprehensive school where the five GCSE pass rate was only 14%. I failed my exams because I didn't have a learning habit. My peer group just didn't care about learning. The irony is, I had two parents who worked in teaching and did care about education.

I chose to retake my exams. It was only because of my interest in tech, software and programming and my love of video games, that I decided I wanted to become a video game developer. I knew that if I was going to do this, I needed to focus on my studies, get my 'A' levels and go to a decent University, which is what I did. I chose the University of Kent because it had

"As a technologist, you can take an idea, start laying down code, build an app or a website, and you can launch it on Google Play or Apple App Store, or publicize your website and get access to a global audience."

an industrial placement year. And through that, I ended up working in an investment banking space, as a software developer. The university also had a program for developing its graduates, and I chose to return and be part of it. I went on to go traveling and did all sorts of wonderful things.

Through being a software developer, I spent over 10 years programming risk and pricing systems in the investment banking world. As a kid from southeast London who never even heard of an investment bank, it was unbelievable to believe I ended up living in Switzerland for five years. My experience and intrigue leapfrogged me forward in life. By leveraging the technical skill set that I've developed and built over the years, I launched a Fintech start-up in 2014, called Neyber. The company raised over 200 million pounds, and we lent out over 170 million pounds to UK-based employees. Neyber was well known for being Goldman Sachs' largest FinTech investment at that time. They invested over 100 million pounds of work through that organization. The fact that I was able to do that was all because of that technical skill set that I had learnt and developed.

INVESTING IN INCLUSION

Most people know me as one of the board, and founding members, principal investor, and CTO for Impact X Capital. This is a venture capital fund that invests in diverse and underrepresented entrepreneurs. What we're trying to do is find those great founders out there and invest in them for both social good, and profit.

When we look at diversity, we mean from the lens of venture capital allocation. So historically, in the UK, 96% of the funding has gone to all white male funding teams, we look at the group of individuals who don't fall into that category, which is something like 57% of the UK population. So, women, ethnic minorities, and diverse populations, typically only receive 4% of all investments.

START-UPS, HOMELESSNESS AND MAKING THE LEAP HAPPEN

I work as an advisor with several different organizations focusing on very different areas. Spring is an endeavor dedicated to accelerating the UK & Ireland's water sector through innovation and collaboration. Albany Group is a risk, technology and intelligence company, and UK Leaders is a not-for-profit community created and governed by IT. Leaders for peers only. My most recent role as Advisor has been with Crisis, a well- known charity trying to end the problem of homelessness, and with a £200m fund, they're now trying to do that through investing in start-ups. They have put together a fully costed budgeted plan for the government to show how we can make this happen. One of the things they decided to do was to set up Venture Studio. A spin off organization that would focus on both investing in start-ups and potentially building them, to end the problem of homelessness. Typically, this is done through a housing first strategy, because that's very much where Crisis says the core problem is.

Ultimately, it comes down to homes, no matter what you do, it almost starts and ends there. To address this, Venture Studio look for start-ups, companies or ideas that can make homes accessible, affordable, and financially possible. I'm pleased to also announce that as of January 2023, I am now a Trustee for Crisis sitting on their board and the Finance and Innovation subcommittee.

TECHNOLOGY AND ADVOCACY

I see technology as a superpower. And I say this to all the start-ups that I speak to, it's actually why I set up Code Untapped, which is a digital skills accelerator. Fundamentally, we would run hackathons, and coding workshops, and connect diverse and underrepresented technologists with the big corporations and enterprises I had strong connections with.

As a technologist, you can take an idea, start laying down code, build an app or a website, and you can launch it on Google Play or Apple App Store, or publicize your website and get access to a global audience. You can then start to generate revenue, and potentially sell your company or raise money. It doesn't mean it's easy or guaranteed but the possibilities are there, and for the first time in history, there are no barriers stopping you from doing it as long as you have the technical skills.

What I love about this process is that kids like me, who grow up in an environment where there are no wealthy people and no one cares about education, can create a product, and have an international presence with the potential to be the next Google. All self- taught, self-developed, starting from scratch simply because of an idea and laying down some code on a laptop. That, for me, is why I love technology and I love advocating for everything I do.

DIVERSE ENTREPRENEURSHIP

I lead on investments, deals and supporting our portfolio and I provide a lot of the advice and guidance around technology either internally or within the companies that we work with. Considering 57% of the population is underrepresented. Our core mission is to increase the number of diverse entrepreneurs. The fund we're raising for now is £100m, however, our real ambition is to raise and deploy over a billion pounds worth of capital over the next 10 years. We can then drive that leap-frogging effect of taking people from a space where they're struggling to build their start-ups to becoming the next set of unicorns and dashboards that we want to see in this country.

Our first portfolio is impressive and has seen us invest in:

• The second black run unicorn company (valued at over $1B)

• A female healthcare company which is now in every major retail outlet and has increased their revenue by ten times over since we spoke to them.

• A mobile phone company that is making handsets more accessible to everyone, by removing the upfront costs and making it easier for people to gain access to high-end devices.

• A company that is making hair care products safer and more accessible to black women across the world.

• The African equivalent to Marvel and DC who have finalized deals with Dark Horse Comics, Nickelodeon, and other organizations, promoting diverse and underrepresented groups in the comic book genre.

The list goes on and that was only our first fund. Imagine what we can do when we close out the £100m fund.

"It's the execution of the idea that makes it real."

SCALING FINANCE INNOVATION

The Centre for Finance, Innovation and Technology (CFIT) was set up following the Kalifa Review of Fintech (2021) to position the United Kingdom as a global leader in financial innovation. CFIT's purpose is to unblock barriers to growth for financial technology by bringing together the best minds from across the UK in order to drive better outcomes for consumers and SMEs. CFIT wants to lead the world in financial innovation, and in doing so, maximise economic growth across all regions of the UK.

I am honoured to take on the position of the first CEO of CFIT and to have the opportunity to make the UK the undisputed leader in Fintech globally. I look forward to working with the financial services, fintech and technology sectors across the UK to drive fintech growth, attract diverse talent into the fintech sector, and ensure better outcomes for consumers and SMEs. The UK is in a unique position with some of the strongest finance technologists in the world and we have an extraordinary opportunity to support this exciting sector and to capitalise on the forward-thinking approach taken by our regulators, government and industry to ensure that its transformative impact is felt by all.

"Just remember, there is no sure-fire way to win. But if you don't play it's guaranteed that you never will."

FAILURE IS THE KEY TO SUCCESS

Ideas are a dime a dozen. I can give you 1000 ideas right now but none of them are making any money. Why? Because I haven't executed on any of them. It's about just giving it a shot. That's really what it comes down to. You have to give it a shot, it's the execution of the idea that makes it real. It's the doers who should be rewarded, not the person who came up with the idea. Quite simply, if you don't try, you'll never succeed.

One of humanity's strengths is the ability to fail and learn from it. Failure teaches us how to be successful. You're free to try and experiment as many times as you can, provided you're willing to put yourself out there and see failure as something you can learn from, and take that learning and repeat it until you hit success.

To see more on
Ezechi Britton MBE

DREA BURBANK

MD-technologist and delinquent savant.

On the surface, Drea Burbank could be considered an inspiration to all women. Not letting her gender dictate her life goals, she's been a published poet, hot yoga buff, and the only female amongst a crew of wildfire fighters facing "scorching walls of flame." It is, however, her insatiable curiosity, physical energy, and mental strength, along with her ability to find solutions to complex issues with compassion and creativity, which demonstrates how she should not only be considered as an inspiration to all women but to all men too.

For the past ten years, Drea has been working on "high tech for hard science" with a group of brilliant colleagues, applying emerging technologies to seemingly unsolvable and intractable problems. They often find that there is a "new key" that can be created to open an "old lock", and their remit is to help the poorest billion people on the planet; those living outside cell phone range, in tropical forests or vital ecosystems. As the founder of Savimbo, Drea's aim is to employ 1 billion small farmers to clean the earth's air within the next decade by paying subsistence farmers in tropical forests directly for the preservation and reforestation of their lands.

She describes herself as a complex book with a simple cover. Raised by religious fundamentalists, homeschooled, with no power or running water, she went on to study high-tech and preventive medicine at Stanford. A remarkable individual, living a remarkable life in a remarkable world.

In Drea's Words...

STAYING CENTERED TO HELP OTHERS

I do all I can to maintain balance in my life. I am a Yogi and have been practicing the art of Bikram Yoga for over 20 years. This type of yoga is referred to as '26 plus two', which is 26 postures performed twice, also known as hot yoga.

The benefits this brings to anyone's life is nothing short of astounding.

Those of us who develop this leapfrog skill are capable of turning our brains off through yoga so that when it starts back up again, it runs faster, clearer, and more efficiently.

I believe that a brain is like a computer. If you run too many programs on it for too long, it starts to slow down, and it doesn't function as effectively. In addressing this issue with focus, we can all bring peace to our minds and balance to our bodies. It is a positive influence in my life and something I recommend to my friends and apply as I engage in all my projects.

THE 'DIFFERENCE' JOURNEY

Over the years it has taken me to arrive at where I am now, I have been observing, learning, and listening. I have collected a group of people, those with a higher consciousness and IQ. They have had this insatiable curiosity about the world, and we have had a shared interest in constructing 'creative play.'

> "I believe that a brain is like a computer. If you run too many programs on it for too long, it starts to slow down, and it doesn't function so effectively."

"Trust gives
the power to
connect and
leapfrog in life."

'Creative play' was all about crafting a workplace where we could work the way we wanted, thinking as we wished, and where ideas were limitless. We started producing an endless series of projects together, and the process enabled us to leapfrog and find solutions that might not otherwise have been seen. People who have these gifts, think very differently from others and see very different, and often, radical solutions to situations that are apparently, 'unsolvable' problems.

A NEW PROBLEM TO SOLVE?

We were approached by four medicine doctors from the Amazon rainforest. They said "can you stop the logging on our lands?" It seemed obvious to me that we should address it as a pro-social project.

When we started to investigate it, we realized that not only could we pay them three times more to protect the region than we could for the loss of trees on the ground, but we could also rebuild the economies in areas of the world outside of cell phone range. Now, for the first time in the history of the non-technological world, the poorest billion people on the planet have the chance to sell their efforts on a global market. Our solution means we can reverse deep-entrenched systemic inequalities and the way globalization has been driving biodiversity loss. That has never happened before.

This solution has not only changed the lives of the people we are currently working with, but it has given us the ability to leapfrog forward and tackle further systemic inequalities. At the same time, it creates the financial inclusion that is long overdue for people who have not had this life option before.

REAL-WORLD IDENTITY

The developed world is struggling with the concept of identity. What is your identity? Does your digital profile match your real-world identity?

The struggle we go through when we are digitized and have a

public and logged profile is not replicated in the developing world. Here, in the developed world, everybody is known, identity is seen or noted, and 'knowing a person' is not a problem. The issue for somebody in the developing world, who is trying to enter or engage with the developed world, is that they don't have a developed digital identity. This then poses questions such as how are these people trusted? Who believes that they exist? How can they be recognized for their work? Bank accounts? Proof of residency, even proof of existing from birth!

I saw two problems:

First, they didn't have an identity in the developed world, so they weren't trusted. (That doesn't mean they are not doing a good job.)

Secondly, timing. If you are a subsistence farmer, you can only sell or eat the food you generate that day or month, and to survive financially, you need to be paid in advance or even on a daily basis. However, large multinational corporations want to pay three to five years later, so the intermediate brokers were paying the farmers and then reselling to the corporations, taking 90% of the profits.

In my opinion, the overarching problem currently affecting tropical forests, is that subsistence farmers in these regions only intersect with extraction economies: logging, mining, and oil exploration. We advocate payment to plant trees!

Unfortunately, those companies are, in reality, the only organizations that are taking the time to figure out how to 'work' in these regions, and they're not doing a lot of good. When it comes to benefitting local economies, they are not penetrating to the ground level because commodity extraction is the primary reason. I don't know if it's just a different mindset or an unwillingness to pay for resources in advance, coupled with the long-term global cost.

MAKING CHANGES HAPPEN IN THE AMAZON

To make changes to address the current model, we have created a mechanism that transacts differently. A trade for the local peoples' time that allows them to get the profits to repair rather than destroy.

Every person that works with us is assigned a bank account as part of the process. Our non-profit status helps a lot with this because it subsidizes this concept of identity, which then legitimizes people and enables transactions.

TRUST IS EARNED

Trust is a priceless attribute, one that is hard-earned. Only through time and by proving that we are trustworthy, by our repeated words and actions and dedication to a worthy cause, should any one of us expect to be trusted.

I hope I set an example of trust in all my actions. To apply attention to all my commitments and make clear, through my words and actions, that I am here to assist positive and sustainable changes. I am committed, and my earned trust is consistent, infinite, unbounded, and true.

> "Show that true self, and others will believe in you."

Trust gives us the power to connect and leapfrog in life. It is a strength that helps to build solid foundations, reflects dedication, and enables progression. Show your true self, and others will believe in you too.

THE PARADIGM SHIFT: NINE TYPES OF INTELLIGENCE

1. Logical
2. Mathematical
3. Linguistic
4. Artistic
5. Musical
6. Interpersonal
7. Intrapersonal
8. Existential/Spiritual
9. Naturalistic

There are different kinds of intelligence, and the concept of the nine types of intelligence has been the key underlying paradigm which has enabled all we have conceived to occur. When we only value logical-mathematical intelligence, we end up with extractive economies and very digitized societies.

Although the nine 'accepted' intelligences still include logical and mathematical, which are the most highly prized in the Western world, there are others, including linguistic intelligence, which I would say is also prized. There are the aesthetic qualities, like artistic and musical intelligences, interpersonal (interaction with yourself) and intrapersonal (interaction with others) intelligences.

Many suggest existential/spiritual intelligence is important, but the one I really like is naturalist intelligence. That is the gift Charles Darwin had, the ability to see patterns in the natural world. When you value that intelligence, you start to see that Indigenous peoples have the other 'intelligences' at an extremely elevated level. They have interpersonal skills that are highly developed. They read body language and communicate actively that way. They have naturalist intelligence, know their world intimately, and have an entire database, a mental library of all the species surrounding them. They have a highly developed central value system (possibly a tenth intelligence!) which we could benefit from, one that is much more holistically oriented.

I believe we need to teach kids to access all nine intelligences, not just logical, mathematical, or linguistic. Currently, we tend to focus heavily on those three in schools. If the school is lucky, they may have a music or arts program, but generally, the arts are devalued. When the other intelligences are ignored, you can't easily employ lateral thinking to bring in really interesting solutions to what is a logical problem.

With these types of intelligence being taught to children and young adult minds through education, there is a real potential for future generations to tap into and unlock this unique set of tools that will give them the ability to Leapfrog in life.

"I believe in a balance. Technology can be beneficial if you access it for a reason, but I also believe it needs to be turned off."

ACCESSING CREATIVE PLAY TO LEAPFROG

If you engage in problem-solving on the ground with Indigenous peoples, you find that they engage in the same way that Google does; they get in a room together and solve the problem as a group in an artistic, playful, and creative way.

As far as enabling access to higher education, I think that by having access to the Internet, people generally tend to self-educate. The big issue is how do we all access the Internet? Now we are solving that problem for the indigenous people too. What we have created is a base layer of humanity that can now bring in creative solutions. We need to start listening to them as they join us.

WHAT CAN BE LEARNED FROM LESS DIGITAL NOISE?

I believe in balance. Technology can be beneficial if you access it for a reason. But I also think it needs to be occasionally switched off! One of the benefits of interacting with Indigenous people is that they know when to turn technology off, because their lives aren't saturated with advertising and social media. They can still feel and notice the clutter it puts into their lives. Consequently, they only want tiny amounts of technology, those elements that help them to live more sustainably. We would do well to learn from them; when to turn the tech off so that the natural world also cleanses our palate.

If we can bring this practice into our own lives and streamline our daily use of excessive, unnecessary technology, this would allow us to leapfrog into an essential daily cleanse. That will assist us in maintaining balance, focus, and overall well-being.

OUR AGENCY PROJECT VALUES

One of our values is to keep in mind that we are a virtual company, and we do high-tech development. We also value that when you have finished work, you get to switch off. If people are working for us, they must be at full capacity and interact with complete attention. We often work over twelve hours a day, six days a week, but there are other options; for example, we let our team pick as many days or hours as they want to work, even if it's two hours a day for five days a week or three days on and four days off. We have no preference. That is because we believe our team members must be allowed to turn off and re-energize to be ready for a full-capacity sprint.

"By having access to the internet, people generally tend to self-educate."

A LEAPFROG IN CONSCIOUSNESS

There is this concept of consciousness which is almost like another dimension. Last year, I worked on a very interesting project to see if we could measure consciousness in the body using biofeedback loops and psychometric analysis.

I think that one of the problems that we have right now is that so many people are working purely on academic, mathematical, or physics projects. For example, one of the guys who works with us is a rocket scientist. As a logical discipline, they are good at metacognition. They know how to 'think about their own thinking' and know where their thinking is at any given time. They can tell when their 'brain computer' is getting slow, and they know how to restart it. But not all of us know how to measure or be aware of our consciousness. I feel that when you have or learn the ability to create and come up with more creative and innovative solutions, it can really expand the conscious mind. I wish we had a better metric for that so that we could optimize it. That is something I would like to see happen. Watch this space!

"Life is about evolution; it is all about how you use the tools you have got."

NATURE, WISDOM, AND THE WILDERNESS

When you watch a Jaguar take down a deer, do you judge the Jaguar for acting according to its nature? You don't.

I feel that there is a part of us that is still wild and somewhat feral. Having compassion for that part of behavior is probably one of the core reasons that we are moving beyond it.

There is a song that I love and listen to often. It sings about a wilderness where birds steal from others, and as these things happen, do you want to be part of the wilderness? Or do you want to be a different kind of person?

Being able to perceive, and have compassion for nature, has enabled me to also move beyond it and act from a different place and know that I am in that place.

"Life is about evolution; it is all about how you use the tools you have got."

To see more on
Drea Burbank

EMBRACE DIGITAL TRANSFORMATION

Recognize the influential power of digital transformation in reshaping processes, products, and services. By leaving behind traditional methods and welcoming disruptive technologies, we enable leapfrogging. Digital transformation is the phoenix of the modern world; it arises from the ashes of traditional practices and takes flight into the horizon of progress, redefining the landscapes of businesses, governments, communities, and individual lives.

> *"The secret of change is to focus all of your energy not on fighting the old, but on building the new."*
>
> *Socrates*

This powerful transformation enables us to leave behind dated methods and embrace disruptive technologies that can propel us forward, leapfrogging over hurdles that once seemed insurmountable.

NATIONAL COUNTRY PROGRAMS

Estonia is another striking example. The country, post its independence from the Soviet Union, embraced digital transformation to leapfrog its public administration. Today, it is known as the world's most advanced digital society.

CORPORATES

Netflix stands as a testament to the power of digital transformation. It leapfrogged the traditional movie rental business model by embracing digital streaming, completely reshaping the entertainment industry.

NEW VENTURES AND STARTUPS

Revolut, a FinTech startup, has used digital transformation to disrupt traditional banking. Their digital-first approach to financial services has allowed them to leapfrog traditional banking infrastructure.

LOCAL COMMUNITY CHANGE

In rural India, the startup NextDrop used digital transformation to tackle water scarcity. By using simple SMS technology, they reshaped water distribution, leapfrogging traditional infrastructural challenges.

INDIVIDUAL PERSONAL

On a personal level, Gary Vaynerchuk utilized the power of digital transformation to turn a traditional wine business into an ecommerce and media empire, demonstrating how embracing digital change can facilitate a leapfrog forward.

Embracing digital transformation is more than a shift in technology. It's about a paradigm shift in thinking, a readiness to abandon old practices, and a commitment to adopting novel, disruptive technologies. As we navigate the path to progress, may we harness the power of digital transformation to leap, not step, towards our future.

DR. RAMAN ATTRI

Coach-to-the-Coaches and Trainers | Teaches Science of Accelerated Achievements | Award-winning Accelerated Learning & Performance Scientist | Author of 50 Books | Brainz Global 500 Corporate Learning Leader

Raman was born into a very poor family in a remote area of India, with no medical or educational facilities. Contracting polio at the age of 6 months, he was left permanently disabled, and is a testament to the human capacity for conquering adversity. Nearly 50 years later, he is considered a leading authority on accelerated learning. He is the founder of GetThereFaster™, a learning platform which aims to disseminate research-based strategies from the science of accelerated learning and achievements.

Recognized as one of the 500 Global Leaders alongside Oprah Winfrey and Gary Vee, he teaches leaders and executives the art and science of how to progress faster in whatever jobs they are in. It has been a long and arduous journey for someone who now teaches speed. His own achievements are proof of his ability to do more things quicker. He holds 2 doctorates, over 100 international educational credentials, has contributed to 125 media features and is author of 50 books of different genres. Recently named one of the most admired global Indians in Passion Vista, Raman has also volunteered as a mentor in 10 educational establishments.

Currently the only speaker in the science of speed in professional and organizational learning, he regards it as a "devastating competitive weapon," and has dedicated his life's work into researching the capabilities of the human mind to speed up learning and performance. At GetThereFaster™ he provides patrons with a range of training courses, coaching sessions, and mentoring programs to get them where they aspire to go - faster.

His philosophy on life and business is an inspirational masterclass focused on the ramifications of failure. He believes failure is positive and can be seen as a valuable lesson if we learn from it. Failure is only to be regarded as a failure if you do not learn from it. Failure needs to be leveraged, and counterintuitively, he believes it should be embraced. He offers a rather visual example of airplane pilots who are constantly and purposefully exposed to flight failures in order to learn and leverage, ultimately making them better pilots.

Listening to Raman speak, it is clear why he is revered as a teacher and master in his trade. He is able to impart his vast knowledge about complex issues into bite size, easily digestible snippets which, in itself, accelerates learning.

"My research found that the organizations that made the most difference had a unique culture which entailed two elements; it was employee centric and involved managerial input to develop the right ecosystem."

Dr Raman in his own words...

FROM ADVERSITY TO ACHIEVEMENT

Contracting polio at the age of 6 months meant I couldn't walk properly or play with other kids. I was tied to a chair most of the time, so had no mobility. The only thing I could really do was to open up books and read. I didn't have a social circle or friends to distract me, so I could always focus on my reading and learning. Being disabled has perhaps been a catalyst for me. I assumed that people were better than me because they didn't need any help or support. I felt that I needed to do things for myself, and that paved the way forward for me to learn faster. I told myself, if I can't walk with my legs, perhaps there is another area where I can walk, and walk faster.

Having experienced the consequences of accelerated learning, I began to be aware that other people were struggling in that area. So, when I started to give advice to businesses and professionals on how to shorten time to maximize proficiency, I realized that it wasn't something that people were being taught. That was when it occurred to me that I could really make a difference. The idea that things can be done more efficiently, and faster focuses on how business leaders can shorten the development time of their employees. I still have that weakness of not being able to walk freely. Nevertheless, I am able to teach leaders how to walk faster in whatever business or profession they are in.

After 20 years of research and 2 doctorates, I can pretty much say that, there is a whole world out there to understand concerning the art and science of shortening time to proficiency and it became my personal mission to compile it all. During my research I came across a master scientist called Jim Collins. He did a 5-year research project which identified the variables that distinguish companies who are good, from companies who make that leap from good to great. I found his book, 'Good to Great' (2001) really inspirational and it became the basis for my own model. I approached a diverse range of organizations to find out how they did things differently, to see if I could create science out of it. Eventually, I was able to create a science of speed which has developed in the foundation of all my work to date.

SHORTENING TIME

I have worked with over 80 world class organizations centering around the concept of shortening time to proficiency and have found that it takes companies a certain amount of time to bring employees up to speed, regardless of their role within the organization. So how do we shorten time and are there any business advantages? There were definitely business advantages as most of the organizations I worked on achieved massive results, both in productivity levels and revenue. For example, a company in the electronics industry was taking around 12 months for their technical staff to come up to speed in regard to productivity and performance. That's a year, which is a pretty long time. However, when they implemented certain strategies,

"The problem is that most organizations equate speed to a mad rush of delivering the project as soon as they can. That's not sustainable speed and will only create short term results."

they were able to shorten that time to about four months. When that is translated to about 400 engineers, the time saved is magnified and amounts to millions of dollars. That's the kind of massive advantage we get when we implement strategies. That particular company, by now must have amassed billions of dollars through the act of shortening time to proficiency.

Research shows us that the time to develop a workforce is roughly 4 - 5 times that which it takes to bring the product to market. If people are developing slowly, then your workforce is already lagging compared to the rate that technology develops at. But if you can learn at speed and understand quickly that your product is going to work in the market, and your workforce is ready to develop it, they can master that technology and launch it ahead of competitors. Of course, competitors will become smarter in due time, and they will launch copies. However, being ahead of the curve means while they are working on the first generation you would possibly already be on the next. Therefore, you get that edge and stay ahead of the market, just by developing your people at a faster rate.

In analyzing why time proficiency is longer, we need to evaluate the difference between organizations which take 2 or 3 years and those that take 3 or 4 months. The organizations which take years will usually have a trigger point when they will say it's too long, we need to shorten it. However, if the time to proficiency is less than 3 or 4 months, organizations typically wouldn't really have the impetus to shorten it.

In this case, the engagement with the concept is more complex, it takes longer for the organization to understand how their dynamics work, what the culture is, what kind of bottleneck they have. It's less visible, but once we pinpoint it, we can understand what's not working, and then put together the program and forces in play to help them systematically bring those parameters down. So, we analyze first, understand all factors lengthening time, for example, technology and culture and then address those gaps with either training or changing the infrastructure and then implement a standardized program.

When looking at companies and how they deal with time it is culture that is the most fundamental underlying strategy to getting such massive benefits from shortening time. So, bringing that kind of science to an organization requires a culture of change. Leadership and management need to be aligned in order to build that kind of speed. The problem is that most organizations equate speed to a mad rush of delivering the project as soon as they can. That's not sustainable speed and will only create short term results. It also puts a lot of pressure on leaders and employees. However, my research found that the organizations that made the most difference had a unique culture which entailed two elements; it was employee centric and involved managerial input to develop the right ecosystem. It's basically these two elements within the culture which supports the change.

CULTURE AND INFRASTRUCTURE

Although I have a background in engineering, technology is a very small part of it, it's the ecosystem which matters most. Many organizations we have worked with don't have the right kind of technologies to look at the data regarding the length of time employees and managers take to deliver their job to an acceptable standard. In this case, it's impossible to reduce the time it takes to become proficient because we don't know what we are chasing. In this case, we advise on what kind of technology tracking mechanism they need to implement. Apart from that, it's the ecosystem which is paramount, the strategy is based on the thinking process. Most organizations deliver training programs that might help, but that's not necessarily the whole answer to the solution, because training can only help you with a little readiness. It's not going to make you a star performer. It is really more about adopting the right kind of infrastructure and ecosystem.

The model doesn't necessarily have to remain within the realm of business, as the philosophy can be expanded on. For example, in Singapore, the culture and infrastructure are developed so that everything is aligned to each other, they do not contradict or conflict in terms of goals. This is the fundamental science behind time to proficiency because if you do not align everything to the target goal, you're never going to be there in a shorter time. Singapore achieves their goals in super-fast time in areas such as education, or their response to the pandemic. It's the third richest country in the world, because from a cultural and strategic point of view, they save lots of time, and that equals wealth.

A GLOBAL LEAPFROG

The world has started moving faster, which also means the time to learn something, to perform better and produce something great is squeezed. At the same time, customer, societal and business expectations are scaling up. So that means businesses have to attain a level of excellence at an exponential rate. This means the business context is becoming challenging in how we can create excellence in leadership.

In the corporate world, there is a lot more emphasis on time management, but by simply managing time, you cannot necessarily save it. Even if you do manage to save time, that doesn't make you an excellent performer at an accelerated rate or in a shorter time, the actual performance is always going to take some time. The concept of speed is about how soon you can get to a point where you deliver the right outcome the first time.

It is not about getting people to do tasks faster, that's not sustainable. Its competitive speed which allows you to produce products and services across time. So, time directly does not come into the equation because time is the driver. But when we push for more things to be done in a given amount of time, that's not the speed we are talking about here because that is very short term.

The world is not predictable anymore, therefore, the traditional training built for known events is no longer valid because there are a lot of unexpected things happening, so rule-based things are not going to work. I may not be able to train you on situations, but what I can train you on is a thinking process. Preparing you for the unforeseen using principle-based learning rather than content-based learning.

"The world has started moving faster, which also means the time to learn something, to perform better and produce something great is squeezed."

To see more on
Dr. Raman Attri

MOSTAFA SALAMEH

Founder & CEO MSA
Author | Everest Summit Climber

As one of just 20 people in the world to have completed the Explorers Grand Slam of mountaineering and polar adventure, Mostafa is indeed in a league of his own. He has climbed the highest seven summits in the world, including Everest and Kilimanjaro, and skied across the South Pole, North Pole, and Greenland. This is an extraordinary feat in its own right, but considering Mostafa came from a Palestinian refugee family, this accomplishment becomes even more incredible.

After the Gulf War, Mostafa moved to Jordan. The family's financial situation prevented him from attending university, so he started working as a waiter. However, fate intervened, and the young Mostafa was offered a position working for the Jordanian Ambassador in London. After a year, he left the Ambassador but stayed in London, learning English by watching Sesame Street and working in a busy restaurant washing dishes.

After five years of working and playing hard, he started a Degree in International Hospitality and Tourism at Queen Margaret

University in Scotland. However, the dream of managing his own luxury hotel was sidelined when he had a very real and vivid dream, a revelation and a spiritual intervention perhaps. The Palestinian-Jordanian who had adopted the trappings of a liberal, western lifestyle, dreamed that he was on top of the world reciting the call to prayer. This was a turning point where his faith, life, and direction changed dramatically.

It was a strange vision to have since he had no knowledge or experience of mountaineering. Nevertheless, he was committed to working hard in order to fulfill his quest. Determination and self-discipline are powerful qualities, and Mostafa spent most of his time reading books and articles about Everest, polar adventures, and other people's climbing experiences. He initially had two failed attempts in 2005 and 2007, but in 2008, on Independence Day in Jordan, he reached the summit of Mount Everest.

That extraordinary achievement was followed by other expeditions and a knighthood before Mostafa returned to Scotland, this time to do a Masters Degree in outdoor education studies. Once he completed his 7th summit, he then skied across the North Pole, South Pole, and Greenland and has since been given an honorary doctorate from Queen Margaret University.

Today he is an explorer, inspirational speaker, fundraiser, and author. His first book, Dreams of a Refugee, published in 2016, documents his life, accomplishments, faith, and commitment to Islam. Based in Dubai with his wife, it is not a surprise to learn that their home enjoys a direct view of the tallest building in the world, the Burj Khalifa.

"I often say that everyone has their own Everest to climb, whether it's work, family, education etc."

Mostafa in his own words...

DISCIPLINE DELIVERS

In 1997, when I had just moved to Scotland, a close friend gave me a book called The Alchemist by Paulo Coelho and it totally changed my perspective. One part of the book that has always remained with me, is that everyone has treasure to discover, but in order to find it you have to be passionate and never give up the search. So when I had my dream in 2004, where I stood at the top of the world, I woke up at 3am in a cold sweat, and knew that was my treasure.

I was 34 years old then and had found my purpose and that was to climb. However, I soon realized that there are a number of elements which come together to make climbing and polar adventure happen. The most important element is mental, it makes up 70% of everything needed. The other 30% is divided equally and includes the physical, technical and financial elements. For example, when I'm climbing up to 1000m, and there is 200m left and I just can't move my body, it takes will power to get me up and going. Physically, I'm exhausted, but my brain is telling me "listen, you've trained so hard you did everything you can do. Why are you stopping? Keep going". So I keep going. It's this psychological aspect, self discipline, inner strength, and an iron will which come together to pull me up that mountain. In contrast, if I had a technical problem, or my body just wasn't physically fit enough, then I would have to turn around and come back down, regardless of will power.

> "My adventure company has completed 60 expeditions in the Himalayas, Africa, Europe and South America. We have also managed to raise millions of dollars for charity, this is really my biggest achievement."

The mental element isn't just emotional resilience and willpower, it's also discipline, that sense of self-control which delivers the outcome. For example, whatever I am doing or wherever I am, I will stick to my regime. I go to sleep at 10pm, get up at 5am, meditate, train, and stick to a good diet. It's not just about sticking to a training regime, part of discipline involves believing in yourself, and your ability, and to keep that faith in yourself even during failure. If I don't believe in myself, then no one else will. From the King of Jordan, to sponsors like Range Rover, Turkish Airlines, or Shell, in order for them to believe in me, I need to have that self belief first because I am acting as their ambassador.

LEAPFROGGING

When I first wanted to get support, nobody really believed in my idea. I thought about explorers like Christopher Columbus, who targeted royalty and got the attention of Queen Isabella, who in fact sold her gold crown to support his journey of exploration and adventure. I thought I would do something similar and go directly to Jordanian Royalty. I researched the King of Jordan and noticed that he liked to read The Sunday Times. So, I managed to get in touch with the newspaper's editor, and they published an article, Climate for Peace. Ten days later, I received a phone call from His Majesty's office. That could definitely be considered a leapfrog moment because, without that patronage, it would have been very difficult to accomplish what I did. Having support from King Abdullah II leapfrogged me closer to my mission. He also knighted me and wrote the foreword for my book Dreams of a Refugee. Moreover, his advocacy led others to sponsor me, which was a game changer.

EVEREST VS. KETU

I often say that everyone has their own Everest to climb, whether it's work, family, education, etc.., but personally, when talking specifically about mountains, it's not Everest that is the hardest to climb. It's K2. At 8,611m above sea level, it's the second highest mountain next to Everest, which is 8,848.86m above sea level, but K2 is, without a doubt, the hardest to climb. Although climbing Everest takes time, there is a lot of help for you. There's a rope from Base Camp all the way to the top. People are carrying your stuff, erecting your tent, and the staff are cooking your food. The only thing you need is to have money to pay for it all and the ability to walk. At K2 or even Annapurna, you don't have any of that assistance. In my experience, K2 can be more challenging and more dangerous.

DREAM-MAKER

My adventure company has completed 60 expeditions in the Himalayas, Africa, Europe, and South America. We have also managed to raise millions of dollars for charity, and this is really my biggest achievement. However, taking people for the first time to climb a mountain is also exciting for me because it makes people's dreams come true. And especially people from the Middle East because it wasn't part of the culture until recently.

I always ask the climbers the reason they want to climb and if they are happy to fundraise money for charities. It usually takes one year of planning and preparation before we climb, and I give them a shortened lesson of everything I have learned in the past 17 years, things like what they should take with them and the best brands to buy.

The training program only takes a few months. You don't have to be super fit. Just being fairly fit is enough to climb a mountain. It's also not about the altitude; it's about the attitude because it's a spiritual journey. You take yourself out of your comfort zone to somewhere that you have never been before.

When you come back down, you have a newfound appreciation of your life and the environment. You realize how small you are, just a tiny dot compared to this massive mountain. I always tell people to treat this mountain as their house of prayer. It doesn't matter what religion you are, just treat it with respect. If you do that, you can definitely make the summit.

THE GOOD FORTUNE OF DUBAI

I have been in Dubai for the past two years. It's a place full of conferences, so there are many networking opportunities, and networking often leads to stuff happening. I have just started something called The Summit of Hospitality, which is a series of talks and training sessions for five-star hotels around the Gulf and the Middle East. It's been very successful as I am able to bring lots of aspects between climbing mountains, polar adventure, and hospitality.

Fortunately, a lot of people in the Middle East now want to climb mountains, it's become very popular, especially Kilimanjaro or Everest Base Camp, as they're not too big. In Dubai, I try to encourage CEOs, big organizations, or public figures to come and climb, so every year, we get big teams climbing, and it's a great way to raise money for charities. We also have lots of private schools coming each year to climb and fundraise. Since Dubai is an international city, there are a lot of opportunities.

I do many talks in schools because we have published a number of books for children which aim to teach the new generation about outdoor education. My books are now part of the Jordanian Ministry of Education curriculum and are available in schools in Qatar and Turkey. I also visit refugee camps in Turkey, Syria, and Lebanon. I am truly passionate about giving children the hope and determination to succeed.

"The mental element isn't just emotional resilience and will power, it's also discipline, that sense of self-control which delivers the outcome."

PROJECTS AND DREAMS

My next project is called 777 for Palestine. I am going to run 7 marathons in 7 days, on 7 continents. My project also aims to showcase and promote Palestinian food, culture, and literature because I want people to be able to see the personality of Palestine. I'm in training at the moment. I'm not a marathon runner, but I've been training for the past year, and the plan is to run a marathon every 24 hours in a different continent. So starting from Antarctica, then to Africa, then Perth in Australia, Dubai in the Middle East. I also want to go to Asia, Europe, and America. That is my project.

My dream would be to do 3 things to change the world to make it a better place. Firstly, it would be to change all governments, secondly I would ensure that everyone had a high quality of education, and thirdly I would like to see the world come together. But I ultimately think that with any change we make, we have to start with ourselves, and then try to change everything else.

> "I ultimately think that any change we're going to make we have to start with ourselves and then try to change everything else."

To see more on
Mostafa Salameh

HARNESS LOCAL SOLUTIONS

Utilize local knowledge, assets, and talents to devise leapfrogging strategies that cater to a community's unique challenges and opportunities. This approach allows us to design new paths that are custom-made to local needs. Our roots hold the power of local wisdom, a reservoir of knowledge and expertise, uniquely suited to solving the challenges that lie within our immediate surroundings. Harnessing this potential can create powerful leapfrogging strategies, ones that are attuned to the unique characteristics of a community and its environment.

"There is nothing like returning to a place that remains unchanged to find the ways in which you yourself have altered."

Nelson Mandela

NATIONAL COUNTRY PROGRAMS

In Brazil, the government's Bolsa Familia program utilized local knowledge to address poverty. Rather than adopting one-size-fits-all solutions, it focused on delivering tailored financial aid to families, effectively leapfrogging traditional social aid challenges.

CORPORATES

A stellar example of this approach is Safaricom, a Kenyan company, which developed M-Pesa, a mobile money transfer service. Safaricom recognized the lack of traditional banking infrastructure and the widespread use of mobile phones in Kenya. It used this local understanding to create a service that transformed the financial landscape, leapfrogging traditional banking hurdles.

NEW VENTURES AND STARTUPS

Sehat Kahani, a Pakistani telemedicine startup, is another example of local problem-solving. The company connects female doctors, who are often unable to work in traditional healthcare settings, to patients in remote areas. Their innovative model leapfrogs the traditional healthcare infrastructure limitations.

LOCAL COMMUNITY CHANGE

In rural Rwanda, local communities developed OffGridBox, a solar panel system that provides electricity and clean water. This solution, designed with local resources and know-how, leapfrogs traditional infrastructure challenges.

INDIVIDUAL PERSONAL

On a personal level, Malala Yousafzai used her local knowledge and experiences to leapfrog traditional barriers for girls' education. She created the Malala Fund, which works on a community level to advocate for and deliver girls' education in regions where it is often neglected.

Tapping into local solutions is not just about addressing local needs, but also about valuing and celebrating the unique knowledge, skills, and experiences within our communities. As we journey toward leapfrogging, let us keep in mind the potential that lies within our local landscapes to fuel our forward leaps.

ADAM RIDGWAY

CEO – ONE MOTO

Adam Ridgway set up his first company when he was still at school. After a number of successful projects, his passion for sustainability found an outlet with his award-winning, impact-driven EV ecosystem, ONE MOTO. It was born from a "random inquisitive mindset" and is set to change the way we move around with less impact on the environment.

Although he's not from an engineering background, Adam nevertheless holds a huge amount of technical and statistical information, claiming that motorcycles are 16 times more harmful to the environment than SUVs or buses. What Tesla has achieved with the motorcar, ONE MOTO aims to match with the motorcycle.

As a successful entrepreneur, Adam has built four businesses over the past 14 years. He regards himself as a spontaneous and creative person who has led a very full life. After extensive travel, he has finally settled in Dubai and spends his time skydiving, playing gigs around the world, and most importantly, being a husband and a father.

Despite starting his first business as a 16-year-old schoolboy and setting up several companies in branding, design and strategy by the age of 19, he feels that it took him a while to find his footing, as he didn't really know "where [he] belonged in the world until [his] late 20s." By the time he was 23 years old, he had led an international property company before moving into the world of television. It's an impressive CV by any standard, but especially for someone so young. The world of TV presented him with boundless opportunities, allowing him to travel, meet incredible people, party with celebrities, jam with rockstars and learn how to present himself in any social situation.

He now seeks to pass on his experience, knowledge and wisdom of entrepreneurship and help potential founders to achieve greatness.

In Adam's own words...

LEAPFROGGING TECHNOLOGY

I was fortunate to have a classic car several years ago, which I wanted to get converted to electric. I went to 3 garages, and they all said they could do it, but all failed. Upon exiting the last garage, I saw a spectrum of beaten up and battered petrol delivery motorcycles and wondered where electric delivery bikes existed. Being an avid biker for most of my life, I started to look into it locally, regionally, and internationally, to no avail. But the tenacity of the question had me thinking. So I conjured up a few trusted contacts and started exploring.

Initially, I reached out to several customers to find out what they needed from a delivery bike. Then with my network, we started to explore, design, strategize and develop the ultimate vehicle that could not be superseded by technological advancements. This became the origins of the ONE MOTO concept: iconic electric motorcycles and bikes. And within 18 months, the vehicles were certified and on the roads. We were pioneers in our field, battling against the naysayers, and we were first to market and first to start educating people about the benefits. The journey had only just begun, and wow, was it an adventure.

> "I have a portfolio of successful and failed start-ups, ideas, projects and investments, so experience tells me that with failure comes learning."

THE EV REVOLUTION

"The problem today, as great as it may be, won't be there in a month. You just have to navigate through it in bite-sized pieces."

The good fortune of timing and being best in class has led to traction internationally. The vision and execution were soaked up from the years spent building brands for others. We wanted to be as sustainable as we possibly could and to ensure our supply chain mirrored this. Of course, walking is the most sustainable act of mobility, but that isn't necessarily convenient. Although lithium production has its negatives regarding the planet, it's arguably better than combustion engine vehicles and the components. Taking our vehicles' technology, we use far fewer parts in the configuration, which results in the end product being more sustainable from production to operation.

The advances in technology will, of course, lead to iterations of our vehicles, and they've been designed to accommodate this as the energy sources also advance. This will hopefully lead to greater ranges, cleaner production, faster speeds, and more affordability. We are now focused on ensuring affordability, and in the UK, we can lease out our vehicles for just £3 per day.

Petrol motorcycles produce 50 times more hydrocarbons than SUVs and Buses. The 92,000 vehicles in Dubai alone are producing 245,000 tonnes of CO_2 each year, killing over 290,000 acres of forest annually (that's just 92,000, there are 30 million in India, 20 million in Pakistan, and 1.3 million in the UK). It's an inconceivable amount when you look at it on a global scale, so our Mission is to decarbonize all last-mile vehicles in the UAE by 2025. We're on track, but it takes collaboration.

MINDSET IS CRUCIAL

I believe most of the world is tired from the fear-mongering that surrounds sustainability, however, the science stacks up. We need a collective mindset, and with each of us doing our small bit to bring about change, things can improve.

The mass adoption of EVs has been mainly European led through incentives, but this isn't sustainable. Private companies need to change their mindset and work alongside the public sector to create opportunities to trigger the traction necessary for other countries to follow. It's happening already, but more needs to be done.

I have a portfolio of successful and failed start-ups, ideas, projects, and investments, so experience tells me that with failure comes learning. Mindset is so important, and it's crucial that any collaborators share the same attitude. When I approached potential investors in the early days, they couldn't understand what ONE MOTO was about. On reflection, although I had a vision, I shouldn't have expected everyone to understand it. Today, I do things a bit differently, and instead of *telling* people about ONE MOTO, I *show* them what it's all about.

TAKING SMALL STEPS

Being a founder, you traverse phases of your personal life, blending your business into your own world to a point where you can't focus. The good times are sensational, but the low times can seem to last forever. However, there's a nugget of wisdom I hold close during these times, "the problem today, as great as it may be, won't be there in a month." You just have to navigate through it in bite-sized pieces.

Mental well-being deserves its place in everyone's life. The freedom and clarity of mind we gain through exercise is crucial and facilitates both our personal and professional lives. I struggle with prioritizing time. My family, wife, friends,

and work are all equally important, but so is 'me time.' This is the easiest to sacrifice, yet holds an equal value.

To help me take the small steps, I've onboarded one of my most trusted mentors, David Cook, A spirited human being and running partner, and a man I hold with family regard. Each morning at 7am we run 5kms, with two sets of compound exercises, and he asks me for the three things I am going to achieve that day, and I ask him the same question. Having a trusted buddy to work out with is far better than hiring a Personal Trainer, and it is more motivating as you're both accountable to each other. This is my regime, it's 45 minutes, and it has transformed me. Regardless of the stage you are at, you shouldn't put yourself under pressure to join a gym, commit to anything long term, or spend a single dollar. Just do a little bit often, and you'll convince yourself it works.

GIVING BACK

At the start of this year, I grabbed my sketch pad and scribbled a series of 'wants'. I had no expectations of what I was going to illustrate, yet what had bounced out of the page was 'looking for Adam', the man I had lost sight of. Reflecting on what brings me meaning, fulfillment, and empowerment made me realize that I wanted to give something back. So this led me to create a platform called www.onefoundertoanother. com, which is dedicated to guiding founders, entrepreneurs and business owners to navigate challenges, topics, and issues around business decisions. Since launching this year, I've helped and supported many founders in the UAE, UK and Australia cross-sectors and introduced them to my international network of specialists.

KNOWING WHAT'S IMPORTANT

In many ways, the pandemic unified the world and forced us all to look out for each other and ourselves. It made us slow down, take stock of what is important and ignore the noise.

Each of us needs to approach life for what it is, an adventure. For the first 20 years, you are learning who you are, and for the last 20 years, you are reaping the benefits of the foundation you laid. The middle part of the trilogy is what really matters. And what does matter? That is up to each individual to answer. Is it financial freedom? Leaving the world in a better place than you left it? Passing on assets, wealth, or estate? Raising a family loaded with virtues and values? Whatever your driver, find that one thing you love, do it well, and give it everything you've got for as long as you can. That, to me, is success.

Money or assets are not my drivers. Although I am interested in making a profit and the financial freedom it facilitates, for me, the driver is the deal, the signing of a contract, the confidence gained from delivering something great.

> "Whatever your driver, find that one thing you love, do it well, and give it everything you've got for as long as you can. That to me is success."

To see more on
Adam Ridgway

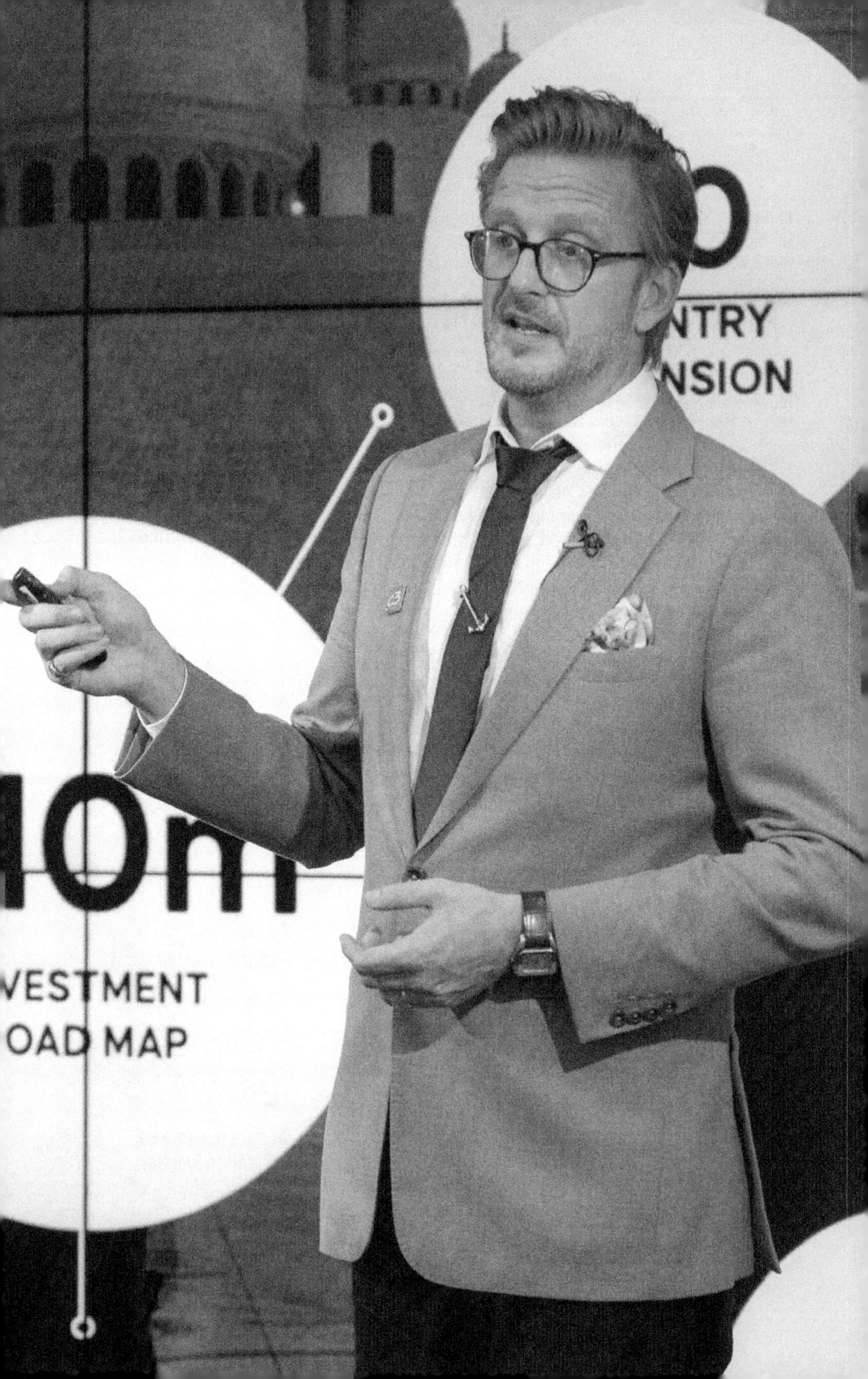

DEVON HARRIS

Original Jamaican bobsledder,
Motivational speaker, and author

From a young boy running barefoot races in a Caribbean "ghetto" to a triple Olympian and one of the first members of the Jamaican bobsleigh team, Devon has certainly lived a life worth documenting. Swapping middle distance running in a tropical climate for speeding 90 miles an hour down narrow, twisting ice tracks in a gravity-powered sled, it's no surprise that Disney chose to dramatize his journey with the adventure comedy Cool Runnings. However, this turning point brought him more than just fame, it gave him a platform and a global audience to share all the lessons his journey from sun to snow had to offer. He now lives in New York with his wife and five children. It's no surprise that people queue up to see him speak, he is animated, full of energy, motivation, and passion, with a tinge of his Jamaican accent, a continual reminder of his journey.

Growing up, Devon was a typical boy interested in sports and the army. What wasn't typical was his tenacious spirit and steadfast belief that the universe had more to offer him than life in "one of the toughest ghettos in the world." Devon's first leapfrog

"Daring to dream can get you everything."

was joining the army, something that allowed him to escape the poverty of his upbringing and develop the leadership, discipline, and persistence that he attributes much of his eventual success to.

As the first Jamaican bob sledding team to reach the Olympics in 1988, Devon has helped pave the way for future generations of Jamaicans to dream big, beyond their wildest dreams and self-imposed limitations. The determination and imagination necessary for a triumph of this scale captured not just the imagination of a country but the whole world.

Devon in his own words...

LEAPFROGGING

Since adolescence, I have always wanted to be in the army, so as soon as I was old enough, I applied to be an officer. The selection process was one of the most grueling experiences of my life. Three long and arduous days were spent competing for a position, so I was overjoyed when 33 candidates were eventually whittled down to just three, which included me. Then a brutal 18 weeks of basic training ensued. Regardless of the immense challenge for someone so young, my childhood dream was realized, and in May 1986, at the age of 20, I took my first trip out of Jamaica to the Royal Military Academy in Sandhurst, UK. I was a kid from one of the toughest ghettos in the world, and I found myself strolling the lawns of one of the most prestigious military training schools in the world. It was a major leapfrog that had a life-changing impact.

Daring to dream can get you everything, and as a middle distance runner, I dared to dream that I was going to be the next Sebastian Coe. It dawned on me when I was very young that these athletes that I idolized weren't, in fact, superhuman, they were just like everyone else, except they had extraordinary dreams and the extraordinary desire to pursue those dreams. I was truly inspired, and I just thought that if I dreamed big enough and worked hard enough, I too could become an Olympian.

> "A big part of leapfrogging is recognizing that when an opportunity presents itself to you, you have to grasp it with both hands."

A big part of leapfrogging is recognizing that when an opportunity presents itself to you, you have to grasp it with both hands. So, when I set my goal to enter the Olympics, I was excited to have been offered the opportunity to go to the teen trials for the bobsled team. I was army fit but not sports fit, I was a middle distance runner, and bobsleighers are sprinters. But I was determined, I worked hard and smiled a lot, and I got selected.

We all, at one time or another, reach a crossroads in life where an opportunity presents itself and requires you to step out of your comfort zone and face your fears. On the first day of the team selection, we were shown footage of horrific, spectacular crashes and people getting killed. The next day, only half the squad turned up. So, even though I am scared of speed and height, I made the bobsleigh team, and with only 4 months to train before the Olympics, I left the warm, sunny climes of Jamaica for the freezing, icy temperatures of Calgary. We were a team of 4, myself, Dudley and Chris Stokes, and Michael White. It wasn't our bobsleighing skills that leapfrogged us into the Olympics, it was our belief in ourselves.

This event led to another leapfrog moment, with Disney making a film about the team. It's flattering on one level, but kind of inspirational too. The idea that you have to work hard to reach your full potential and that being your best can motivate others is a worthy tale to tell. Since the film was released, I have had so many people from around the world express how much the story in the film has mentored them. It also introduces me to new generations, and with my role as a motivational speaker, that can only be a good thing.

MENTORSHIP

I have had a few mentors throughout my life, teachers who have encouraged me, national heroes like Samuel Sharp who inspired me, and real life heroes like my commanding officer, Colonel Alan Douglas, who had the insight to suggest I bobsleigh. However, there was one person in particular who had the most impact on my life. Loretta Robinson was the most amazing storyteller, grandmother, mentor, and possibly the one responsible for how

> "The idea that you have to work hard to reach your full potential and that being your best can motivate others is a worthy tale to tell."

my life has unfolded. Without her stories about soldiers performing amazing feats, I may not have had the dream to join the army. Without her capturing my 5-year-old imagination, I may not have developed the tenacity and perseverance to pursue the impossible. Without her sharing her wisdom and time, I may have lived a very different life.

GIVING BACK

I believe success principles are universal. Although you may not have the very same background and upbringing as I did, the challenges may be similar. So as a public speaker, I think I bring a sense of authenticity. Bob sledding and the film have given me a platform, but my experience and the lessons I have learned along the way should be shared, so I can help others. I teach life and health skills and conflict resolution in about 24 countries around the world.

I also founded the Keep on Pushing Foundation to provide practical solutions to some of the obstacles faced in educating kids in disadvantaged communities. We have a primary school with a breakfast program and a supply program, and we have also helped 10 other schools with resources.

BEST PRACTICE

There have been a number of practices I adopted when I was young that have stayed with me. When I wake up in the morning, I like to quiet my mind through meditation and visualizing my goals, which presently

are to expand on my foundation, write a best-selling book, and do more traveling. I'm particularly interested in going to places I haven't visited before, Australia is on my list, as is Iceland to see the aurora borealis.

LEAPFROG FOR THE WORLD

The biggest leapfrog for mankind would be to show care and be empathetic to your fellow man. If everyone could do everything with a little more kindness, it would leapfrog us into an entirely different space. If we look around any part of the world, there is constant conflict, inequity, and suffering. Plenty of times, those who are in a position to help just don't see the humanity in others, but if we developed more empathy, we'd all be better off.

WISDOM TO LEAPFROG

Learn to use your existing skills, knowledge, and experience to create new opportunities for yourself. The biggest lesson I learned is not that I could learn to bobsleigh in a very short period of time, but rather that you could literally accomplish anything in life that you truly set your mind to.

To see more on
Devon Harris

ENCOURAGE COLLABORATION FOR SHARED IMPACT

Promote collaboration and partnerships across various sectors, disciplines, and places. Pooling resources, expertise, and networks can result in a greater collective impact, helping to shape new paths together. We live in an interconnected world, and in today's age of complex problems, no one person, company, or country can go it alone. Collaboration and partnerships are vital ingredients for success, the kind of success that creates a greater shared impact and paves the way for leapfrogging together.

"Alone we can do so little;
together we can do so much."

Helen Keller

NATIONAL COUNTRY PROGRAMS

The Transcontinental Railroad in the USA stands as a historic example of collaboration for shared impact. The collaboration between multiple stakeholders—government, laborers, engineers, and investors—made it possible to connect the country and leapfrogged the existing transportation systems.

CORPORATES

One excellent example of this comes from IBM and Apple, two tech titans who once were competitors. They chose to collaborate, combining IBM's big data and analytics capabilities with Apple's consumer experience, to develop mobile apps for enterprises. This partnership leapfrogged the competition, delivering innovative solutions faster and more effectively.

NEW VENTURES AND STARTUPS

In the startup world, there's a partnership between FarmCrowdy and Twiga Foods, a Nigerian and a Kenyan agritech startup, respectively. They combined their expertise to bridge gaps in the agricultural value chain, leapfrogging over traditional agriculture challenges.

LOCAL COMMUNITY CHANGE

The Solar Sister initiative in Africa is a testament to the power of collaboration at the local level. It brings together women from different communities to form a network that promotes clean energy solutions, leapfrogging over traditional energy constraints.

INDIVIDUAL PERSONAL

Nobel laureate Muhammad Yunus, founder of Grameen Bank, leveraged partnerships between borrowers, usually impoverished women, to create a peer-lending model that leapfrogged traditional banking barriers.

Encouraging collaboration for shared impact allows us to pool our resources, strengths, and ideas to create solutions that are more robust, effective, and sustainable. As we move forward on our leapfrogging journey, let's remember the power of 'we' over 'I'.

DR. AMINE AREZKI

Director Marketing & Communications – Thales

With a Ph.D. in robotics, Dr. Amine Arezki is not your typical science genius. He uses his creative and business acumen to create practical things for the common good. Even his robotic dog, which may initially seem like a fun moment of self-indulgence, sets to answer important questions - what benefit does it have for society?

At the time iXeraBot, the so-called dog who could walk, dance, and kick a football, hadn't yet directly benefited many people apart from Amine himself, who grew in confidence, not just in his ability to create a robot but also in his ability to convince sponsors to hand over the money for him to do so. However, from little acorns grow mighty oaks, and the question of benefit soon came into play during the pandemic when the 3d printed robot dog led Amine to co-found amaskforall.com offering free printable masks.

The perpetual question about what benefit something has for society has colored Amine's sense of being. He has been involved in a number of projects, from helping stroke victims regain mobility to autonomous, greener rail travel, both endeavors striving to benefit society as a whole.

Holding an Executive MBA from London Business School and listed worldwide as a TOP 100 Executive MBA by Poets&Quants, Amine can use his expertise in both disciplines to design solutions for the future. Born in Algeria, he is now a global citizen with professional and educational links to Germany, France, the UK, and the US. However, growing up in war-torn Algeria has left an indelible mark on him. A young mind negotiating the horror of civil war, terrorism, and indiscriminate bombing, he lost out on a carefree childhood most of us take for granted.

Today, he has made up for much of the precarious existence he endured. Apart from playing the piano, Amine enjoys driving, sculpting from clay, playing football, basketball, and tennis. The key to his happiness is to diversify.

As a Robotician and Marketing Strategist, he is currently working for Thales as Director of Marketing and Communications. He is responsible for the global organization and management of an international and diverse team, with an impressive turnover of $1billion. Amine uses his knowledge and skills in technology and business to share innovation with other organizations to ultimately benefit society.

Amine in his own words...

DESIGNING ROBOTS

When I initially worked in robotics, I was part of a team of 'roboticians' participating in the European Open, a global robot-building competition based in Europe where the end game was to solve a problem. We had to develop a robot which would be fully autonomous in order to solve a specific problem. The problem would be rudimentary, such as grabbing, catching, or shooting something. Our team had very limited funds available, so we had to think creatively and create something simple, but still, ours actually ranked second or vice-champion. Countries like France, Germany, and Italy created very complex robots but

> "Robotics isn't necessarily the creation of something complex to solve a problem. You can simplify things and target the problem, and this is the concept that I use even today on different projects."

did not win because they were not solving the problem. Robotics isn't necessarily the creation of something complex to solve a problem. You can simplify things and target the problem. This is the concept that I use even today on different projects.

"I like to challenge myself, push boundaries and diversify."

ROBOTICS TO LEAPFROG REHABILITATION

In 2008, I worked for a US research lab helping stroke patients who had been left disabled. Working alongside physiotherapists, the goal was to provide motivation for rehabilitation. Because it affects the brain, a stroke can change the victims' behavior, so it's important to stimulate them into doing simple tasks. My contribution was designing a solution to push them into doing their exercises, which entailed a combination of robotics and video games. Basically, virtual reality encouraged them to do very simple things. For example, depending on which part of the body had been affected, the premise was for them to play a game, picking up an object, or following a particular path. Because it was a video game where they aimed to reach levels and get a score, it was more motivational than just exercising.

After a set of trials, it was patented. Now the technology is being developed further and is showing real benefits and quicker recovery times for stroke patients. Hopefully, this will help more people.

RAILBOT: A GAME CHANGING IDEA

I like to challenge myself, push boundaries, and diversify. I don't want to do the same thing repeatedly, so more recently, I have emerged from the lab into transport. Autonomous trains are perhaps the largest robots in the world, and it's been a very different experience because I have needed to do a lot of work behind the scenes before getting the thing off the ground. Marketing, strategizing, getting funding, etc.., which I now do, are all very different from working in a research lab. However, it has proved extremely rewarding as it has resulted in getting one of the first autonomous train projects up and running in Europe. First in France and now Germany. The Railbot is a combination, a robot that runs on rails, and it's something I am incredibly proud of because it is a game changer for the industry and thousands of commuters.

RELEVANT QUESTIONS GET RELEVANT ANSWERS

Organizations often invite me to speak, and one thing I always do is learn about the specific company I am speaking at. When I do my workshops, I am able to ask the questions I feel are relevant, get valuable feedback and an accurate understanding of the product, market, and competitors. When you have a deeper understanding of the issue, you already have half the answer. Listening to people within the organization allows you to get experience to help the company effectively. For example, when working with some organizations and dealing with a mainly technological arena, the challenge is understanding the points of concern and then trying to orient them in different directions to find a solution. When you are dealing with people who are experts in that domain, they are usually biased. They often need convincing of what actually needs to be done. These are my favorite types of workshops because this is where I can challenge them, and guide them, to find the solutions themselves.

AI HAS ARRIVED

Today, there is far too much emphasis on work, productivity, and money, and people should now be thinking differently. We are advancing rapidly with robotics and Artificial Intelligence, and many people are seriously afraid of these technologies. But AI is already with us, and it's everywhere in our systems, already working and helping us to function. People should not be scared because they are already using it, and if we learn to market these tools in a different way, people will be more accepting and begin to use these advancements more.

AI will continue evolving and will either replace specific roles, enhance other roles, or give today's worker a different role tomorrow. There will also be an economic change, and we need to think about what AI and robots are generating today and how that can benefit future society.

I regard myself as a marketer, and because of my background in technology, I'm only too aware that both disciplines are bound to merge with the development of AI. Marketing is not like it was 10 years ago. It is all about AI, augmented reality, and virtual reality. The technology is extremely complex, and traditional marketers will struggle to understand it. Personally, I feel empowered by having an in-depth knowledge of both disciplines. It allows me to leapfrog the way we are doing things in Thales, especially in terms of the way we advertise and are now using different technologies.

THE EXPERIENCE OF WAR ON PERSPECTIVE

The concept of creating something huge

from nothing is perhaps ingrained in me. My father is a neurologist based in Algeria, and he has been creating the most extensive neurology department in the country. My mother is a physiotherapist and was a basketball captain for the Women's Algerian team. In Algeria at the time, that was quite a bold and open pathway for a woman. My parents were both considered intellectuals, which was not a particularly good thing to be in Algeria during the 90s. However, I think with my upbringing of challenging the status quo, being progressive and intellectual while navigating difficult situations has made an impact on my perspective and behavior. I am emotionally resilient and constantly challenge myself because of the surroundings I grew up in.

Coming from the chaos and danger of a civil war, I feel very fortunate for what I have today. As I grew up in Algeria in the 90s, there was always this feeling that you could lose someone you love or even your own life at any moment. Going about your normal everyday business, going to the shops, coming back from school, or from playing football, you knew a bomb could go off at any time. When you have experienced that closeness with death, you see problems differently. You don't tend to panic. You simply see them as something that needs to be solved and just a part of life.

Because of this experience, I feel I am in a position to help others wherever it is possible and perhaps empower them in some way or help them to grow or accomplish a project.

LEAPFROG TO CHANGE THE WORLD

Helping someone else is the best feeling.

> "I feel very fortunate coming from the chaos and danger of a civil war to what I have today. As I grew up in Algeria in the 90s there was always this feeling that you could lose someone you love, or your own life at any moment."

To see more on
Dr. Amine Arezki

DR. LEON VANSTONE

Rocket scientist, storyteller, idiot!

It's not rocket science! But it is to Leon Vanstone, an expert in experimental rockets, hypersonic, and scramjet technology. He founded the University of Texas Rocket Engineering Lab and is known to introduce himself as a rocket scientist, storyteller, and idiot. He demonstrates a good sense of humor but also has a passion for communicating the wonder of the universe.

For Dr. Leon, the best scientists are always great storytellers, as he believes when people are inspired by stories, they will do fantastic things. That is why he credits storytelling as a major contributor to the successes he has had in his career. Growing up watching Star Trek, Leon loved the way the science fiction series provided a lens into future technologies, many of which have now come to light. Flip phones, for example, were directly influenced by the Star Trek communicator. He hasn't stopped looking into the future, driverless cars, vactrains, moon bases, and space travel. He is an agenda contributor for the World Economic Forum, an active member of Austin Global Shapers, and on the Board of The Dumpster Project, an innovative STEM education platform to create tiny sustainable homes from trash dumpsters.

As for being an idiot - it is because he understands that the more he learns, the more he realizes how little he knows. It's probably because his work looks at how to stop things that are traveling exceptionally fast through the atmosphere from melting - now that is rocket science! It is an important job and requires an innate superpower. Even when he is not doing it, he's talking about it.

In his spare time, Leon embraces the simple life. He enjoys crafting things with wood, DIY, and even a bit of axe throwing. He takes on projects simply to learn how things work - he once bought all the components for a drone to make one. His lectures on Tedx evidence his humor, passion, determination, and his mission to make the world a better place.

DR Leon in his own words...

LEAPFROGGING IN SPACE

A rocket is a terrible engine. It is one of the most inefficient in the entire human technology portfolio. You would only ever use one if you absolutely had to. Imagine you are in a car and it's a dragster. You redline the engine from the starting line and roar off with the goal of getting to the top of a hill. As you go, you are rapidly drinking through your fuel until you run out. But you still need to make it the rest of the way up the hill, so you start unbolting pieces of the car and leaving them at the roadside until you eventually roll to the top in nothing but a frame with four wheels and the seat.

That is pretty much how rockets work. We start with a huge tower of mainly fuel sections and end up with a little capsule having 'thrown away' most of it. Then there is the cost, which of course, is enormous. The leapfrog technology to help solve some of these issues and the area I work in is called hypersonics - the ability to fly at incredible speeds when you are still within the atmosphere and then basically throw yourself out into space.

> "Failure and success are two sides of the same coin. They are inseparable. You don't just start and only succeed; you fail a bunch of times until you finally achieve success."

As well as hypersonics, there are other ideas to reduce the waste and costs in space flight. Reaction Engines is a very interesting company, UK-based, and they are working towards what is known as a 'single stage to orbit' vehicle. Think of it as a space plane - the Shuttle was a stepping-stone to that. A hypersonic plane is a single vehicle that takes off intact, goes to space, deploys cargo, then comes back down to Earth, lands, and gets refueled, just like an airplane.

That's the dream, anyway.

FUTURE SCIENCE

Technology is completely agnostic. It has no view on whether or not it was built specifically for space. One of my favorite examples of space technology leapfrogging other sectors comes from the Hubble telescope project. At first, the lens was very blurry, so they built algorithms to fix the blurriness, and those algorithms ended up in MRI machines to make pictures sharper. Ultimately improving diagnosis and saving lives.

"Things happen really quickly on social media and in the movies - like Tony Stark making breakthroughs in his basement - but in the real world, scientists scurry around for years before any kind of advancement is made."

In another area, there are now many new satellites going up which creates new constellations to map GPS from, and that is going to be very enabling. Most people are not aware, but one of the things the GPS network does is provide a very tight timing network to the whole world, and because of that, 5G is possible without a relay. The GPS network provides a timing for that – the 5G revolution would be impossible without GPS.

As space becomes more affordable and accessible, we are going to see tourism, but we are also going to have the ability to move more mass up into space and will have to decide what manufacturing technology we will take up. You see, the future is an exciting prospect.

SCIENCE AND THE NEXT GENERATION

Things happen quickly on social media and in the movies - like Tony Stark making breakthroughs in his basement - but in the real world, scientists scurry around for years before any kind of advancement is made.

Consider Nobel Prize-winning scientists who have made some enormous breakthroughs. It has taken years of work. They didn't suddenly have one massive idea, they had years and years of small improvements, and then, eventually, something tangible was created.

I have found that, especially when teaching, the best way is to show people. It is very hard to just tell someone they can be great. Think of a kid with their first bicycle. You tell them not to worry, they can do it, but as they have never ridden a bicycle before, it's intimidating. They may spend a lot of time procrastinating just to avoid getting on it, so you put the stabilizers on and let them go. Later, when a little more confident and enjoying the ride, the stabilizers are removed and they fall off, but as long as they keep getting back on, they will get there in the end.

The point is failure and success are two sides of the same coin. They are inseparable. You don't just start and only succeed; you fail a bunch of times until you finally achieve success. You just have to keep doing it. You simply can't give up.

What I do to motivate young people is create little microcosms of time where someone focuses on a project for a week and gets something at the end of it. Then they see it working. Next, we'll try for a month and see what happens.

PROBLEM-SOLVING WITH A COMMUNITY

NASA has had its share of unsolved problems, some they had been working on for 60 years. One day, someone very smart persuaded the organization's top officials to release a list of these conundrums to the public. Shockingly, some were then resolved within three months.

I love NASA, with all of its brilliant technical expertise, but at that moment I learned that when you involve the community and devote more time to your problem, you always end up with more science. If you can get 10,000 people to work an hour on a problem, results will follow. And that is because of the diversity of the group. An issue in one field has often been solved elsewhere for an entirely different reason or purpose, but we just did not know about it.

INSPIRING THE NEXT GENERATION

Most people have never had the expectation set that they can be brilliant, and that what they do can positively affect the world. Whether that lack of ambition is down to society, their community, school, or their parents, it doesn't matter. If they are shown that they can be brilliant, lives could be changed.

The Rocket Lab I started at the University of Texas was about proving that anyone can be a rocket scientist. It's not hard. Mentally, once you've cleared that hurdle, you just keep going and moving forward.

AN IDEA TO CHANGE THE WORLD: ROBOTS

100,000 years ago, our ancestors were all subsistence hunter-gatherers; we foraged for food while on the move. About 10,000 years ago, we saw the first subsistence farmers cultivating food for our communities while a few kings and priests got to spend time doing science, art, and cultural things. Fast-forward to modern times and barely anyone forages for food. In the United States, only 3% of the population grow food for its 360 million people, whilst the other 97% of people contribute to science, culture, art, and enterprise endeavors. This is relevant because people are concerned about robots coming into the workforce.

Take self-driving cars - in the US, there are six million people involved in the transportation industry. Within a decade, robots will have taken over that skill set. This cycle has been the same throughout all of human existence, jobs come and go, and we need to see it as a positive and enable people to retrain and make the most of the opportunity. The robotic world and advanced technology are coming whether we like it or not.

My view of robotics and AI is that they will remove menial labor and menial thought from human tasks, freeing people to engage in science and enterprise and fulfilling things for mankind, where we, as communities, can turn to each other. Much more of our basic life will be taken care of for us, and people will be more free to go out into their community and ask how can they help, how can they make life better, how can they change the world. Once we see more of that, I believe society will improve dramatically.

> "Success and failure are two sides of the same coin."

To see more on
Dr. Leon Vanstone

PRIORITIZE HUMAN-CENTRIC DESIGN

Keep the needs, dreams, and values of people and communities at the forefront when planning leapfrogging initiatives. This way, we ensure that solutions are impactful, user-friendly, and inclusive. At the heart of every remarkable leapfrogging initiative lies a profound understanding of people - their needs, dreams, and values. After all, what is innovation if not an endeavor to enhance human life and to make it more fulfilling?

"Design is not just what it looks like and feels like. Design is how it works."

Socrates

NATIONAL COUNTRY PROGRAMS

The national healthcare program in Denmark is a remarkable example of human-centric design. The patient's needs and preferences are given priority, ensuring the delivery of healthcare services is not just effective, but also considerate of the patient's dignity and comfort.

CORPORATES

Apple Inc., one of the world's leading technology companies, is renowned for its human-centric design. Their intuitive user interface and attractive design aesthetics, developed around the user's needs, allowed them to leapfrog their competition, setting a new benchmark in the tech industry.

NEW VENTURES AND STARTUPS

Airbnb, the vacation rental startup, was built with a profound understanding of its users' needs. By prioritizing human-centric design, they have revolutionized the hospitality industry, leapfrogging traditional hotel booking systems.

LOCAL COMMUNITY CHANGE

In Colombia, the Escuela Nueva (New School) model revolutionized rural education. By adapting the curriculum and teaching methodologies to the local context and children's realities, they achieved significant progress, leapfrogging traditional education constraints.

INDIVIDUAL PERSONAL

Engineer Arunachalam Muruganantham's invention of a low-cost sanitary pad-making machine in India is a compelling instance of human-centric design. By keeping the needs and economic limitations of rural women at the forefront, he leapfrogged traditional barriers in women's health and hygiene.

Prioritizing human-centric design is not just an approach; it's a philosophy that places people at the core of all initiatives. Let's keep this at the forefront, ensuring our leapfrogging solutions are impactful, user-friendly, and inclusive.

SUHAIL JOUANEH

CEO at Better Business

Suhail likes to introduce himself as a "dental surgeon by profession, but a mindset surgeon by passion." However, there is a more inspirational element to this lighthearted enigma, as after 11 years working in the dental industry, Suhail had the courage and foresight to pivot his career path from the medical sphere into business consultation.

It is clear that what he enjoys best is "helping people to help themselves," particularly working with business leaders to support them in fulfilling their true potential. There are a variety of puns he likes to use to express his career change, "going out of the tooth and into the mind" is just one of them, but joking aside, for more than 20 years, Suhail has been focused firmly on the human factor.

As co-owner and CEO of Better Business, he provides solutions for companies seeking to develop their employees, grow their business, and achieve sustainability. He also heads up Learning and Development and to date, has organized 1000s of workshops and trained over 25000 people from more than 40 countries around the globe.

Based in Jordan, when Suhail has time to himself, he loves researching and developing processes and inventions that serve humanity. His leisure time also consists of reading, trekking around the world, and exploring with friends.

Suhail in his own words...

A BOLD CAREER SHIFT

When I first shifted careers from dental surgery to consulting and training, I started volunteering my services in developing countries to help people grow their potential. I was supporting leaders with all kinds of skills, and it was a real eye-opener, even a heart-opener because it made me understand that diversity and inclusion are vital to good leadership.

I used to be picky in terms of who I connected with and the people I chose to have around me, but after working with so many different cultures, I completely changed my outlook. The experience made me realize that humanity means dealing with any human being on Earth. That was an important lesson I learned, and it came to me gradually and not always that easily.

Leaders are also human beings, and they should reflect this in their leadership style. It is this simple and rather obvious acknowledgment that has made me into a more flexible person who can work with a diverse range of people and with sometimes difficult cases. However, on reflection, my experience in developing countries has been an excellent training exercise, and it's something I am always conscious of in my work today.

DIVERSITY AND INCLUSION

I am keen to embed diversity and inclusion as part of my consultation and training package. It is a process that took some time to develop, but I am now reaping the rewards, mainly

> "Leaders are, in fact, human beings, and they should reflect this in their leadership style."

because people are looking towards a future of unity as opposed to a future of separation.

Culture sets the stage and the context for everything we do, and the concept of diversity and inclusion in the Arab world is primarily based on religion, region, and relatives. People are categorized on the basis of what religion they are, what region they live in, and where their relatives originate from. Although things are changing, I think there is still an element of bias in the Arab culture with regard to a person's educational background, appearance, age, and gender, all of which can affect employability opportunities. Positive changes are occurring now, with Governments in the Arab countries trying to fix these perspectives. With more people like me becoming learning facilitators with awareness regarding diversity and inclusion, I think things will change rapidly.

> "A successful business starts with good self awareness and social awareness, which affords you the ability to know not only yourself, but the people around you."

EMOTIONAL INTELLIGENCE

Working in my leadership sessions, I like to start from an inspirational perspective. In fact, this is my specialty. I do a lot of emotional intelligence sessions with leaders, and many of them spend time discussing different things amongst each other. I am there to listen. The process helps them look at different perspectives. I still meet leaders that I worked with years ago who tell me they still remember the discussion sessions we had and even do exercises from them. The sessions can be pretty impactful.

I recently delivered a course for 60 leaders from Bank Al Etihad in Jordan, which included intervention exercises, assignments, coaching sessions, one-on-one interaction, encouragement, and even WhatsApp coaching. Afterward, the head of retail came to me and asked what I did to the people because they had changed. Even the people working under the leadership expressed how much their managers had changed. I put my heart and passion into helping people because this is part of my psyche, and it's great to learn of its impact.

BECOME A LISTENER TO LEAPFROG

A successful business starts with good self-awareness and social awareness, which affords you the ability to know not only yourself but the people around you. This kind of acknowledgment informs your reactions, mood, psyche, and emotions. It can also help in managing different relationships.

With developed self and social awareness, problems and relationships are well managed, and the business ultimately grows in the right direction. It's not all necessarily about business; some people have personal objectives, and I help them because I have a humanistic approach to what I do. It is possible to help individuals achieve both their own personal goals, as well as improve organizational objectives.

Our problem is that we don't listen to people carefully. I have only recently started to read articles about how listening in leadership is a major skill, and it wasn't something that was focused on before. But now we need to get back to basics and understand that fundamentally, for any relationship in the world to succeed, we need to learn how to listen to people and listen attentively. Because whenever I listen, and actually hear, I start to know the person better. I also get to know myself better. It is only when we are silent that we learn. We rarely learn when we talk.

STARS OF SCIENCE

I was hired as a coach for the finalists on 'Stars of Science,' a television competition promoting technological innovations which improve communities. For the series, my primary role focused on developing contestants' self-confidence. These were people who had terrific inventions, and they needed support in being able to communicate quite complex information to the judges and viewers. This meant they needed to pitch their ideas with clarity and confidence.

Teaching them was fundamentally a simple matter of repetition. They repeated their pitch over and over until they developed the confidence to do it on TV. It's not something that comes spontaneously to most people, even naturally charismatic people need to rehearse in order to start using the right words. My workshops were on an individual basis where I could give them one to one support, and it was really getting them used to using the right words to express accurately what was in their heart and mind.

PRESENTATION SKILLS: SHOW YOUR VALUE

Many people make the mistake of focusing on themselves when doing pitches or presentations, which usually results in the audience turning off. If presenters focus on achievements and accomplishments instead, people will be naturally more interested. For example, we don't do anything entirely on our own, even if it's just a matter of being inspired by a word or a sentence which goes toward our path to success. When presenting to people, it's good to acknowledge that, be down to earth, and focus on accomplishments and influences rather than yourself.

There is a fine line between talking about yourself, risking putting people off, and talking about your abilities so people believe in you. However, not talking about yourself too much doesn't mean you have to appear too humble. You need to know your value and, moreover, show your value, and that comes from being able to talk about your work accomplishments. I meet a lot of people who purposely underestimate themselves to show modesty and humility. But this can, unfortunately, fire back. If you are not able to demonstrate to people your capabilities and accomplishments, then people won't invest in you.

NANO LEARNING AND MINI BITES

Before March 2020, I wasn't even considering technology in my work, not even Zoom. Covid changed all that, and now technology has become part of our methodology. About 18 months ago, we launched our eLearning platform to focus on business and help HR departments implement self-paced training courses. The space is a personal development plan where people can keep growing anytime, anywhere, and it's more cost-effective. We've had to change our mindsets a great deal and are now investing in that platform because it's the future. People want nano learning and mini bites.

Many people say that Artificial Intelligence is a great thing, and I am sure there will be many positive outcomes from it, but, like most people, I don't want to see AI replace humans. Big Data and the Internet of Things will no doubt change consumer behavior, but we still need human interaction, and I will fight for that.

HUMAN PURPOSE

Every person on earth is here for a purpose, and when we know our purpose, we start finding the right direction in life. When we discover that direction, we need to embrace it and live with it until it becomes part of our system. For example, when I look at my personal vision statement, it states, I am here to help people. I know that I have a role in building people's lives, influencing them, and helping them to unleash their potential. I know for a fact that I exist for that. I want to change people's mindsets and how they think, so they can grow themselves and create great things out of their lives.

If you appreciate that you are the average of the five people you spend most of your time with, it will make you choose those people more carefully to ensure you are with people who lift you up and see your potential, not the people who only give you nice words and pat you on the back. You want to be with people who can benefit you, talk to people who can feed your mind with helpful ideas and ideologies, and build you up. You want to listen to those people, be their companion, and stick to them. You want them as your mentors. Even without you asking their permission, you can have them on your side.

> "Every person on earth is here for a purpose, and when we know our purpose, we start finding the right direction in life."

MY LEAPFROG FOR THE WORLD

Humanity needs to be protected, as the future of mankind shouldn't revolve around technology. Instead, it should focus on a change in human behavior because we need more altruism. For me, it's one of the highest values of humankind. I would like to see a world where everybody is ready to help everybody else, where everybody thinks of everybody else. And this is how we will start to live as true human beings. For me, a more altruistic world would be the best global leapfrog for civilization.

To see more on
Suhail Jouaneh

SAEL
AL WAARY

Acting Group Chief Executive Officer at Bank ABC
(Arab Banking Corporation B.S.C)

As a banker and technologist Sael Al Waary is at the epicenter of banking transformation and Fintech. A seasoned public speaker, he advocates for change within the banking sector and embraces innovative ways to lead in the digital world. Sael is a man with passion; he has a passion for change, and a passion to make a real impact. It's important that he can help people, and he manages to do that through innovation. As the founder of the Fintech forum MEA, he brings together leaders to discuss future trends and challenges within the industry, so he has his eye firmly fixed on the big picture and always looking ahead to the next big thing. In his role as Group CEO of ABC Bank, he has ensured that the Bank's strategy has innovation at its core. He is committed to building the bank of the future, and one of the ways that he plans to achieve this is through a set of principles; most importantly, agile decision making, embracing change and innovation, driven by AI and data analytics.

Impactful and Relevant are the words Mr Al Waary mostly connects with. A seasoned banker, he has remained dedicated to the same organization throughout his career, rising to each new challenge and opportunity provided across the Bank's global network from Hong Kong to New York, Milan and London. Starting as a Group IT Director, then Group Support Head, moving up to Group Chief Operating Officer before becoming Deputy Group Chief Executive Officer and now Group CEO.

Under his leadership during 2022, Bank ABC recorded $1b in revenue for the first time in its history and also won 12 banking awards for its various endeavors. However, Sael still remains humble in light of such success, and believes there is a lot more work still to be done. Preferring action over words, he doesn't often speak about himself, but nevertheless, his achievements speak for themselves.

Sael in his own words...

FOLLOW YOUR PASSION

Through my dedication and constant search for new ways to create positive change and impact, I have been able to grow within the organization throughout my career. As long as I remain relevant to those people around me, and I am helping them by mentoring and pushing them to achieve their potential, then I am content. I once read a book by Jack Welch called 'The Winning'. It's a book about management and business, and in it, he said that you should 'find your passion and follow it. Do what you love and do what you like.' And that is how I live my life. I am passionate about what I do, which is probably the reason I have been with the bank for so long.

LEAPFROGGING

When you have an innovative and disruptive idea, before you can launch it, you need to first start by getting your stakeholders to buy-in to the concept. My strategy is to selectively enhance, leapfrog and disrupt our propositions to stay ahead of the competition. When the Fintech disruption started in the GCC in 2016, my vision was to introduce a new seamless way

> "Passion inspires. Find your passion and follow it, that is how I live my life."

> **"My strategy is to enhance, leapfrog and disrupt in order to jump ahead of the competition."**

of digital banking. I consulted with subject matter experts, industry disruptors and close friends to research and plan before going to my Board and introducing them to fintech and the digital disruption of financial services and securing directional approval. I then hosted a session with subject matter experts to raise awareness and educate the Board as to the future of banking and digital disruption. Finally, I presented a proposal for digital investment including the digital, mobile-only bank proposition and successfully secured the Board's support and funding. So leapfrogging is not an overnight process. You need to first make sure that the stakeholders understand fully what you are aiming to achieve, the value of leapfrogging the competition. You have to have a clear vision, fully understand your goals and make sure you are well-prepared to answer any questions and convince others.

Digital banking is really about delivering a new customer experience. Anybody can build a better looking app than you, but they cannot compete with your vision and the customer experience that you can provide. In order to move away from legacy systems and take steps towards modern Banking and financial services, I brought in the technology which allowed me to embrace the ecosystem, by adopting cloud computing.

You have to understand your customers, looking at smartphone penetration in the GCC, it has steadily increased reaching about 200%. This means that before launching ila, (our digital, mobile-only retail bank) we basically had all the ingredients to introduce mobile banking, smart banking and payments. Because of familiarity with the internet, digital banking is not such a cultural shock, in fact, I think people were more than ready for it.

ila BANK

In 2019, we launched ila Bank (in Arabic 'ila' means 'to'), and it was a huge success because people were already familiar with smart banking and digital banking etc. The introduction of contactless payments and wallets, where you just tap and go has changed the behavior of the Arab citizens and Arab society in general. The launch of ila bank, coincided with the outbreak of the covid pandemic and I initially panicked that the pandemic might affect the roll-out but we found that customer acquisition surged exceeding all KPIs and expectations, because people couldn't physically go the Bank and after a period of time, they no longer wanted to go back to traditional banking. They could just open a bank account while at home in lockdown. So digital mobile banking and payment systems have accelerated behavior change. Today, if you look at the percentage of transactions done online, it's probably over 10 times more than that in 2019. The reach of banking services have expanded, people no longer need to go to the bank. Customers can make payments directly through mobile apps. It's become part of everyday life, embedded in the culture of the digital-savvy generation. As digital technologies evolved, customer behavior embraced such advances.

Everything is so convenient these days, for example, my son was recently in Paris and he has an ila bank account. He ran out of euros and I was able to simply transfer him some money within seconds and he could just withdraw it from a nearby ATM. I couldn't have done that so quickly a few years ago. Our lifestyles have changed due to advancements in technology – and the opportunities for Banks and digital services have been accelerated by the covid pandemic. Looking now at the potential of data analytics and AI, I think this is only the beginning, things will continue to change quickly as the digital era has brought different generations closer together and our customers are seeking effortless digital-first solutions.

FINANCIAL INCLUSION

The notion of financial inclusion is close to my heart, especially financial literacy. I have delivered many speeches, including with the United Nations, on how to support marginalized communities to access banking and financial services and increase financial literacy. For people who are underserved and underprivileged, it's very important in our society to give them the tools to access financial services and access and manage their money.

In Bahrain, the Government launched an initiative around 5 years ago to develop a scheme called the Wages Protection Programme digitizing payroll for low-income private sector workers, guaranteeing them regular payment of their salaries digitally through a secure online platform allowing them to open a bank account within 4 minutes, with just two forms of ID, and then they were able to access to their salaries making it easier for them to save money and to send money to their families through digital banking.

We have many initiatives for financial inclusion, it is one of my main goals to serve the 'unbanked and under-banked' population, using the capabilities of our digital, mobile-only ila bank.

It is important from a global perspective to improve financial literacy and highlight the benefits of banks and financial services. Indeed, it is one of my main goals to serve the 'unbanked and under-banked' populations, using the capabilities of our digital, mobile-only ila bank.

AI IS COMING

For the future, I can see AI becoming a major driving factor in the banking sector and the way we live our lives in general. I think banks will eventually become AI banks providing mass individualization and intelligent advisory capabilities to customers. In addition, digital assets will be the next big thing. So your bank account in the future, won't just include your traditional accounts balances, but it will have a secure vault for all of your digital assets.

Speaking about what the future may look like, I would like to see more investment and digitisation in healthcare and education so that these can be delivered anywhere in the world. We have had many successes in the banking sector through digitisation, and now that investment needs to be redirected to developing more accessible therapies, to support better health outcomes.

BEING AGILE

Collaboration is essential for any endeavor. What international forums have taught me is that you cannot do anything on your own. I am fortunate as our home Regulator and stakeholders are open to innovation and willing to take brave decisions in order to disrupt and stay ahead of everyone else. They are constantly leapfrogging, and are one of the best partners a bank can have. The way they have allowed us to disrupt and move into the next generation of banking is a testament to their supportive and agile approach, especially when it comes to innovation or digital advancement. We are fortunate as they embrace new ideas and work collaboratively with us to explore new technologies and innovations.

"What keeps me going after 40 years in business is being able to make an impact and to develop people."

MOTIVATION

What keeps me going after 40 years in business is being able to drive transformational change, make an impact and invest in people. I love to sponsor young talent and see them grow.

I have an eye for talent and am committed to investing in the next generation of leaders. In terms of what keeps me motivated in business, I always want to stay relevant to our customers. To put myself in their shoes a n d develop innovative solutions that improves their lives and businesses. Leveraging my understanding of technology, my passion for change and my determination to deliver on my promises I am never far away from uncovering my next challenge!

**To see more on
Sael Al Waary**

TACKLE INFRASTRUCTURE CHALLENGES

Identify and address infrastructure gaps that could hinder progress. By employing innovative technologies and models, we can bridge these gaps and enable leapfrogging. Navigating the course of progress often requires overcoming physical and technological obstacles. Infrastructure, being the backbone of development, holds the key to unlocking the potentials of leapfrogging strategies.

> *"We shape our buildings;*
> *thereafter they shape us."*
>
> *Winston Churchill*

NATIONAL COUNTRY PROGRAMS

India's nationwide "Digital India" initiative aimed to digitize government services, making them accessible online to its citizens. By tackling infrastructure challenges like internet connectivity, they leapfrogged traditional service delivery methods, bringing about a significant change in governance.

CORPORATES

Apple Inc., one of the world's leading technology companies, iTesla, the American electric vehicle company, tackled infrastructure challenges by creating a network of charging stations, paving the way for the global acceptance of electric vehicles. Their innovation leapfrogged the traditional constraints tied to EV usage, such as range anxiety.

NEW VENTURES AND STARTUPS

Starlink, a venture by SpaceX, aims to provide internet connectivity to remote areas of the world using a constellation of satellites. This ambitious project is leapfrogging traditional telecommunications infrastructure limitations, thereby bridging the digital divide.

LOCAL COMMUNITY CHANGE

In rural Africa, organizations like Off-Grid Electric provide solar energy solutions to communities lacking access to the power grid. By introducing an innovative energy solution, they've leapfrogged traditional energy infrastructure barriers, providing affordable and renewable electricity to thousands.

INDIVIDUAL PERSONAL

Dr. Venkataswamy, the founder of Aravind Eye Care in India, addressed infrastructure challenges in eye care. Through innovations in process and technology, he created a self-sustaining system that has performed millions of eye surgeries, leapfrogging traditional healthcare delivery models.

Tackling infrastructure challenges opens up vast opportunities for leapfrogging. By using innovative technologies and models, we can bridge these gaps, creating new paths for progress and development..

LAMEEN ABDUL MALIK

Founder - 100 Ideas Cafe
Nobel Peace Prize (IAEA) 2005

As part of the International Atomic Energy Agency (IAEA), Lameen was a recipient of the Nobel Peace Prize for ensuring that atomic energy is never used for military purposes. An 'Intellectual Philanthropist' modern leader and a humble, approachable, and engaging human being, he is also regarded as a coffee aficionado.

At the IAEA, he developed a regional strategy to help over 41 African countries use nuclear science and technology to address their primary development challenges in health, agriculture, and radiation safety. With his 100 Ideas Cafe, Lameen continues to spearhead this drive to engage with people from across the globe to find the most innovative ideas to create sustainable opportunities. A simple yet brilliant concept which will bring positive changes and build a better world for generations yet to come.

"The only coffee shop owner to have won the Nobel Peace Prize" was his USP when Lameen ran his own coffee shop in Cape

Town 12 years ago. He is a coffee connoisseur who has written about coffee for over 14 years. His quest for exceptional and, importantly, sustainable coffee, led him to connect with industry giants such as Starbucks and Illy in the hope of improving the coffee value chain.

Sustainability, now more than ever, has become a natural quest amongst those driven to better our world for all. He is a leader with a strong track record of high delivery, with a winning formula based on honesty, competence, fairness, and trust. Perhaps his Golden Nugget could be summed up with his mantra that "Service to others is the rent you pay for your life here on earth."

Lameen Talks About...

USING THE POWER OF HONESTY TO LEAPFROG

I have four strong virtues I live by: justice, courage, wisdom, and chastity. I also aspire to do things in a pure, honest, and transparent way. I like to reflect on the concept of knowledge and to have the courage to try to create change in the world. Life is easier when you are honest and you align that with your thoughts and heart. Using the power of honesty has enabled me to leapfrog in life.

THE POWER OF LEAPFROGGING TO CHANGE A NATION

Winning the Nobel Peace Prize brought with it an award of $1m, which has allowed us to invest in creating a meaningful change in people's lives in Zambia. I was working on a project that would establish the first Cancer Hospital in the country. Of the prize money awarded, $200,000 was allocated to the project, and this contributed towards the training of radiation oncologists, which takes up to four years. The doctors were integral to the hospital and instrumental in treating cancer patients. I am immensely

> "Using the power of honesty has enabled me to leapfrog in life. I find life is easier when you are honest and you align that with your thoughts and heart."

proud to say that the project was successful, and the Hospital Cancer Treatment Centre was opened by the previous President of Zambia in July 2007. Previously, anybody in Zambia who was not wealthy and had been diagnosed with cancer was unable to get the treatment they needed, which sadly resulted in many people dying.

The project's impact has been phenomenal for Zambia. To date, the hospital treats 1500 cancer patients annually. This means that since the center was opened, 22500 people have received treatment that they would not have been able to have without the opening of the center. Not only has the project given an opportunity to the people of Zambia, but it has also extended lives and given people hope and the potential to battle this disease. One of the biggest gifts that the Nobel Peace Prize Award money gave, was the possibility of treating cancer in Africa and fighting for change.

REFRAMING WHAT IT MEANS TO BE A BILLIONAIRE

I want the term billionaire to be reclassified. In my opinion, being a billionaire should not be monetary, it should be about being human and making a difference. My vision is about having a positive impact on one billion people's lives. When I have succeeded, then I would consider myself to be a billionaire.

100 IDEAS CAFÉ - MY PLAN TO CHANGE THE WORLD

I will always subscribe to the concept of future-proofing. When I was working as the Director of a think tank in Saudi Arabia, the CEO asked me to come up with an idea of how we could participate in Expo 2020. I said I wanted to create a project called 100 Ideas Café, a place where people could join us for a coffee at the Expo, and while they drank it, we would ask them, 'Do you have any ideas to impact the world?' I was inspired as to how this one question would help to unite people in creating opportunities

"I want a billionaire to be reclassified, being a billionaire is not monetary, it's about being human and making a difference."

and possibilities for sustainable growth and change which would benefit the world and the future of humanity.

Now, the idea is based on me going to developing countries where people can ask me, 'Lameen, please can you solve my problem?' I tell them, 'All I can do is give you the tools because you're more qualified than me. You live here and know the issues that need solving intimately'. People can often have their own solution, sometimes, it's just a matter of guidance, facilitation, and support to help them to bring out those solutions from within.

I have now developed my idea into three key areas called HER, (health, environmental, and renewables.) I think these fields are the three most important things to consider moving forward in the world. I want to create a safe space on a global scale where anybody can share an idea or show up as a start-up and discuss ideas they have that could impact the world.

HOW IDEAS CAN CREATE THE CHANGE WE HOPE TO SEE IN THE WORLD.

I believe that ideas can come from anybody on the street. You don't have to have a PhD from Oxford, Harvard, or MIT to have a great idea. When I worked with developing countries in Africa, I encouraged people who had great ideas. They're the ones living with their problems on a daily basis. You have the public, you have the problem, and you probably have the solution based on existing skills and experience from many other people in the community. I want the 100 Idea Café to be able to say, 'yes, we can help you with those ideas. Let's see how we can take that forward.'

By 2032 I want every person to have a much better life than we are currently living now. It's not just about having an inspiration or an idea, it's about looking at the vision of an idea, and the future outcome: What skills can people bring? Does the idea have longevity? Is there potential for sustainability? It takes a dedicated committee of people with a variety of experiences to come together to bring new visions to life and make those ideas successful.

LEAPFROGGING TO CHANGE LIVES

In April 2022, we launched a questionnaire under our 100 ideas cafe platforms, where people were encouraged to submit an idea that could impact 1 billion people, using the UN's sustainable development goals on health, the environment, and renewables as a yardstick. My team and I picked the top 10 ideas from start-ups and knew that they would need funding to move forward. With this in mind, I decided to leapfrog ahead and secure my own funding, rather than wait for additional funds to commence the process to impact people's lives. We had our first cohort in September 2022 with 10 start-ups, 8 based in the US, 1 in Thailand, and 1 in Dubai and some have already received funding to bring their ideas to life.

PASSION FUELS INSPIRATION

I have always had a passion for art. It initially started with a love of reading comics like Spider-Man and Hulk as a young child, even creating my own superheroes and occasionally selling my work to family and friends. Almost 20 years later, I adapted my artistic qualities and found new hobbies to inspire me, such as baking, enjoying coffee, and food photography. It's important that in the busy pursuit of daily life, we also need to be doing things that nourish us. It can be so easy to forget sometimes, and it really is so vital. Our passions give us energy and inspiration, and with that comes motivation; this ripple effect leads us to do remarkable things and can bring the potential for leapfrogging into the future of our own lives.

"You can never win a race unless you start it. If you really want to be somewhere you need to start today, tomorrow never comes."

IT STARTS WITH A LEAP OF FAITH

Start now, don't procrastinate. We should look to the future, focus on the grassroots, and take action now towards mobilizing resources, crowdsourcing, and collaboration in order to start working to create better lives for others. You can never win a race if you don't start one, and if you really want to be somewhere, you need to act today: tomorrow never comes.

I appreciate it is not always easy for anyone to quit their job, but I remember a Nugget of wisdom I learned from Steven Foster, Founder of One Golden Nugget. "Don't try, just do. The pathways will begin to open up for you." If we act today, we can have a significant impact on the future and make everyone's tomorrow better. Let's leapfrog with our ideas and start contributing to positive change together.

To see more on
Lameen Abdul Malik

ALEXANDRE JANSSEN

Co-Founder @ Minkowski
Agency for Applied Futures

With a Masters Degree in Communication, Policy and Management, Alexandre considers himself to be an entrepreneur, motivator, futurist, and fundamentally an advocate for building a better future. He admits that he can sometimes live up to the Dutch stereotype of being blunt and direct, but he believes that if you want to bring about change "sometimes you need to be a little bit blunt and direct".

As the co-founder of Minkowski, an agency for applied futures based in the Netherlands, his remit is to create "one million Einsteins within organizations to create better futures." He believes that innovation is not necessarily about ideas, it's really about people. He's been a guest lecturer at several universities, focusing on applied innovation in corporate settings. Speaks 4 languages and has published a number of articles on the concept of innovation.

Before starting his own company, Alexandre's worked for a

global consulting firm, where he co-founded the innovation department. Relaxing is a simple matter of sharing a good bottle of red wine, lounging around listening to jazz.

Alexandre in his own words...

LITTLE STEPS, BIG IMPACT

If you don't believe in something, you will never realize change. And if you want to realize change, you not only need to believe in it, but you need to continuously keep believing in it. And this is something that I do, I believe in making change within organizations. Sometimes that may mean you envision that change isn't going to happen because of all the different variables. But at least you keep your belief and I think that's something that I really stand for, continuously believing that change can happen.

However, despite that continuous belief, quite often people are limited by rules within organizations. So if there is no encouragement for them to try and experience something new, they will never make that step, which could, potentially lead to a big change or difference. I really focus on pushing people to make a little step that can have a tremendous impact. I am a strong believer in a mechanism that can support people in organizations to make that first step in order to make a change. However, to make that first step people need to be empowered to embrace failure, to be allowed to make a mistake within an organization, and that is really down to the company creating a culture whereby mistakes are allowed.

It is more about the principle of having a mechanism that people in a team feel empowered to try something new, knowing that if it goes wrong, they won't get the blame. It's this change in culture which could ultimately bring about a leapfrog moment, which could be big for the company as well as the individual.

> "If you don't believe in something, you will never realize change. And if you want to realize change, you not only need to believe in it, but you need to continuously keep believing in it."

THE 'I F***ED UP' CARD

In my previous work, we had a physical card, it's like a get out of jail free card. It allows you to mess up. Although it's actually a physical card, it's a symbolic reference which reminds employees that they are allowed to mess up. For example, one of my employees gave an interview on the radio about a new service that the company was introducing. Normally, before anything like that happens, employees would have to confirm this with the PR team and the comms department, and ask the CEO for permission. Without the I F***ed Up card, this employee would never have done the interview. It was really good publicity for the company, but it was only because of the culture we had developed which empowered that employee to take a risk and do that radio interview. So the card gives employees the freedom to take risks and make mistakes, knowing that their line managers would support them whatever the outcome. And that's a pretty powerful tool.

We actually did some research with one of the Dutch universities on how this concept could be applied on a team level, or a whole department. It's really an entrepreneurial mindset, where an organization comes up with mechanisms to encourage employees to experiment with new things. For example, some companies came up with the idea of giving away free hours in exchange for new ideas, or giving prizes to people who come up with new experiments. But fundamentally, it's all about the concept of acknowledging that in order to make change, you need to try new things that also can go wrong, and so you should not punish the individuals for it.

"For me, innovation is all about following what I believe in and making a decision and following it, and keeping focused."

INNOVATION AS A MINDSET

I give lectures on innovation, and the word very much depends on the context. For example, what could be considered an innovation for one company could be standard stuff for another. So what is the definition of innovation? The answer is dependent on who looks at it. For me, innovation is a mechanism or the means to get to a goal. Many organizations make the error in seeing innovation as the actual goal itself. The goal is staying relevant in the future, and innovation could be one of the mechanisms to get there, and investing in a different culture, or start-ups could be another way of staying relevant.

So for me, innovation is all about following what I believe in and making a decision and following it, and keeping focused. Most people will say, that's not innovation, but for me it is, because I decided to leave a great job with a big company in order to start something totally new and unpredictable, so I regard that as being innovative. Innovation is really a mindset.

CONE OF POSSIBILITIES

Large budgets don't necessarily make for better innovation. In fact, quite often, a constraint on budget can force people to think differently. It's also becoming increasingly more important to hire people that can look at your business with a different lens. For example, we work with this concept of looking at the cone of possibilities, based on the mathematician Hermann Minkowski's work. This concept is focused on how we explore the different futures ahead.

Our vision is clear when looking ahead, but we can also vaguely see stuff happening on the right and left. As long as we don't focus

on that peripheral vision, it stays vague. So using the cone of possibilities, an organization can broaden their lens and look also at not only the most probable future scenarios, but also the possible and the plausible scenarios. Quite often most people within an organization are "For me, innovation is all about following what I believe in and making a decision and following it, and keeping focused." so focused on the day to day business, that it is very difficult for them to open up and broaden their scope. So I think one of the main things would be to hire people that have different backgrounds and perspectives who can help explore other scenarios.

CREATING A COMPANY CULTURE FIT FOR THE FUTURE

I invest in different startups, so I've witnessed how they start from scratch and either go bankrupt or succeed. So my initial question to start ups is to ask where do you want to be in the future? It could be a wild scenario, but nevertheless, the question forces them to decide what they need and what are the steps that they need to take in order to get there. If they start at the end point, then it's easier for them to stay on that path and focus. There are also a number tips I put forward to ensure a business succeeds. For example, always begin with the end in mind, and make sure that everyone embraces the future endpoint. Be personally involved, work with your clients, not for your clients, co-create and guide them through the journey, that way you give them ownership and so they are more likely to be on side.

Running my own business doesn't seem like work to me. It's something that I really enjoy doing. But what we are trying to do in our organization is to create a culture where people feel that their working day is not necessarily a 9-5, Monday to Friday thing. So our people don't have to ask if they want to take a day off. I believe by giving employees this freedom, where they can just go to the beach if they feel like, it will encourage more commitment, productivity and the basic way they just think about stuff.

Sometimes it's necessary to do nothing in order to come up with new ideas. The same applies for me, I want to be able to take my kids to the zoo on a Wednesday morning if I feel like it. So I think it's being able to have the liberty that when you want to do something else you can and not just relax in the evenings or on the weekends. I see many people looking forward to a summer holiday and I think they must be doing something wrong. If you have to wait until holidays to re-energize then you are obviously doing something wrong.

"I am a strong believer in reverse mentoring, so someone experienced can still learn from younger people in the organization, because they see what's happening from a different perspective."

I had a friend who had a designer who did excellent work but worked best at night, so she would work until 3am and walk into the office at lunchtime. In order for him to allow this to happen, he had to ensure the designer worked in a different part of the building so that colleagues would not see her turning up for work at lunchtime, regardless of what time she finished. The reality is that many managers still don't understand the concept and want people to be in the office, at the same time everyday. It's not in the corporate culture of organizations, so I am really happy when I see young entrepreneurs and new companies adopting a cultural shift. They realize that productivity is not measured on the number of hours you sit behind a computer, which is a really good thing that I want to adopt more in my own company.

I started my career in a corporate environment where you had billable hours, so it's great to see the next generation having totally different demands from their employers. It's not only about salary and pension, but it's about other things as well.

Flexibility for example, whether they want to work from home, or visit friends during the week, come into the office later etc… I have also noticed that young people really want to work for organizations with a purpose, who know what they are doing and why they are doing it. The younger generation have a real sense of activism, and they want that reflected in who they work for. They also want to work for a company where they feel they are equal to others, where it's less hierarchical.

It's important that you create this culture where the employees feel they are trusted and empowered. It's a kind of self-organizing principle, but it also has to be a collaborative process, because the client always needs to be happy, and the process needs to ensure that other colleagues are not impacted.

I am a strong believer in reverse mentoring, so someone experienced can still learn from younger people in the organization, because they see what's happening from a different perspective. It's again, seeing things from a different lens.

KEY SKILLS FOR LEADERS

We spoke to 150 different people around the world from Otto Sharmer to Benjamin Zander to Alexander Osterwalder, and we asked them what are the key skills needed for leaders and organizations to be ready for the different futures ahead of them?

I would love to see world leaders dare to step up and make bold decisions based on what they believe is the best for the world, and not best for their political career. It's not just politicians, CEOs as well need to stand up to the shareholders and sometimes tell them, it's not 6% profit this year, it's 5%. It's about making bold decisions that you believe in.

CHALLENGING THE STATUS-QUO

I was working in a company with 250,000 employees globally, and it was the best learning school ever. But after 10 years in my corporate job, my wife was pregnant with our second child, and I just said to my boss that it was time for me to move on. I didn't have a job to go to, but I knew that I needed to take this next step. It was a risk, but it led to what I am doing now which is building a company, with amazing, happy people, where we can help other organizations build better futures.

My TED talk is all about passionate people making a difference and how difficult it is to be a changemaker in an organization. You need to continuously challenge the status quo and push for change and I really want to see these types of people swimming against the tide being more appreciated, not necessarily financially, but generally more supported when they seek to make changes. I think these are the type of people that will ultimately determine the future of an organization.

"I would love to see world leaders dare to step up and make bold decisions based on what they believe is the best for the world, and not best for their political career."

To see more on
Alexandre Janssen

ADVOCATE FOR DIGITAL INCLUSION

Strive for equal access to digital technologies and connectivity for everyone. This step empowers underrepresented communities and bridges the digital divide, fostering inclusive leapfrogging. In our increasingly connected world, digital inclusion has become paramount. It goes beyond having access to the internet; it's about having the skills and opportunities to interact with the digital world effectively and safely.

"In the digital age, knowledge is power and internet access is a human right."

Anonymous

NATIONAL COUNTRY PROGRAMS

The "Computer for Every Child" program in Israel provides computers to underprivileged families to narrow the digital divide. This national initiative enables access to technology and digital literacy for children, fostering their growth in the digital age.

CORPORATES

Microsoft's "Airband Initiative" is working to bring broadband connectivity to three million people in rural America by 2022. This corporate effort advocates for digital inclusion, ensuring that geography does not limit access to the benefits of the digital age.

NEW VENTURES AND STARTUPS

Andela, a global talent network, empowers African tech talents by connecting them with remote jobs in top global tech companies. This startup advocates for digital inclusion, leapfrogging traditional geographical and economical limitations.

LOCAL COMMUNITY CHANGE

One Laptop Per Child, a non-profit initiative, provides low-cost, connected laptops to children in developing countries. By bridging the digital divide, they are fostering educational opportunities and digital inclusion at a community level.

INDIVIDUAL PERSONAL

Jimmy Wales, the co-founder of Wikipedia, championed digital inclusion by creating an online encyclopedia accessible to all. His personal mission leapfrogged traditional knowledge barriers, democratizing information globally.

Advocating for digital inclusion is more than just bridging the digital divide. It's about fostering an environment where everyone, regardless of their geographical location or socioeconomic status, has the opportunity to benefit from the digital revolution.

CHRISTOPHER COLBERT

Speaker, advisor, innovator, globalist

Speaker, author, innovator and globalist Chris Colbert has been leading the way in business optimization for many years. The son of a four-star admiral in the US Navy, he grew up traveling the world and learning to lead.

At the vanguard of a wide range of national and international companies, from database corporations to consulting firms and advertising, his 'pièce de résistance' has centered on business growth and turnaround strategies. Chris has been particularly involved in supporting leaders within finance, education, and healthcare transformation. He considers these fields to be "the essential enablers of modern society" and as such, reflects his focus on embracing the human truth, challenging ways of thinking, and creating motivating foundations.

In the role of Managing Director at the Harvard Innovation Labs, Chris supervised all departments while working closely with the leadership team to form strategies that would increase reach while improving learning impact and venture outcomes. He considers this work a truly rewarding part of his life, supporting Harvard students and select alumni in their pursuit of exploring the world of innovation and entrepreneurship.

Leaving Harvard and offering his expertise to a wider group, Chris has remained committed to education. And, he became a Board Member and Chief Growth Officer for the School of Humanity, a virtual school with a specific purpose to prepare future generations to be active stewards and engaged, caring citizens. He is now based in the Greater Boston Area and is simply - chriscolbert.com. Traveling extensively and internationally to speak at public events about his insightful perspectives on the human condition and how it connects to a world of global innovation, technology, and stewardship. A published author, his latest book This Is It (2019) is a motivational piece for those with the desire, but not the impetus to change the trajectory of their life.

An erudite individual, and progressive thinker, Chris is able to wear many different hats demonstrating a wide range of skills. But first and foremost, he is an innovator, capable of finding simple solutions to complex problems in order to unleash the unrealized potential for organizations, countries, and individuals.

Chris in his own words...

PROFIT VS. PEOPLE

Increasingly there are two camps in the world. The 'Techno utopians' who believe the world is progressing in excellent form, enabled by technology that is driving global productivity. This camp's optimistic approach is dependent on the standard measures used for defining economic success, which provides evidence that things are indeed improving. For example, we know the poverty rate is declining, and the longevity of life is increasing. However, the other camp isn't so optimistic, suggesting that these standard (economic) measures are missing the point, and I tend to agree. Focusing purely on economic productivity is inherently flawed because it doesn't take into consideration the concept of

> "Focusing purely on economic productivity is inherently flawed, because it doesn't take into consideration the concept of human satisfaction, human aspiration, and the realization of the full potential of the individual as a whole."

human satisfaction, human aspiration, and the realization of the full potential of the individual as a whole.

Focusing on economic productivity alone, without reference to longevity versus wellbeing, satisfaction, and contentment, doesn't give us an accurate picture. Using economic measures as a barometer also fails to realize the full entity as a country or as a planet. So if you asked me what the biggest leapfrog we can make as a species is, it would be to reset our intention.

There is definitely a demand among employees, especially the Millennials and Gen-Z, for more than just financial reward, they are looking for purpose, and they want the companies they work for to share that need for purpose. Seeking more than just mere financial profitability, they desire to work for companies that want to deliver something back to the community and the world. The younger generation in the workforce are looking for companies that have created an environment that is motivating and fulfilling, one that allows people to realize their full potential. For most corporations, the intention is largely economic, and we need to consider that the lessons for corporations are not that different from those for countries or the planet.

COMPASSIONATE CAPITALISM

Capitalism and technology have converged, and it's become this pure play profit thing. Companies and countries need to reset their intentions beyond economic productivity. I believe in capitalism, but altruistic capitalism or humanistic capitalism is the right approach.

"If you ask me what is the biggest leapfrog we can make as a species, it would be to reset our intention."

As leaders, our job is to excite people, to motivate them to reach beyond their natural tendencies and realize their full potential. By doing so, this will realize the entity's potential, whether it's a company or a country. In America, our politicians have been consistently failing to provide any kind of motivating, or even unifying context, and there's an issue with partisanship, at least in large chunks of the Western world, which needs to be addressed.

There are countries around the world that are beginning to understand that the essential factor of our existence is our humanness, and that it has to be more than just GDP and economic growth. Certain European countries, for instance, use other metrics to measure success beyond economic productivity, and that's good news, but that creates its own issues with the complexities involved. Regardless of the issues, we still need to find ways of measuring more accurately what is meant by success and accept that it is not how much wealth we're creating, it's what kind of lives we are creating for ourselves and each other.

EDUCATION, EDUCATION, EDUCATION

The only way to save humanity from itself is to educate humanity. We are grossly under-educated for a world that is exponentially changing on a daily basis. The education system in the United States and beyond is woefully out of sync with the needs, demands, and realities of how the world works today. If you want to create a high-performing company, you need to create a high-performing country and a high-performing world.

In order to do this, we need to overhaul our education system. Changing how the system works, measuring its efficacy, delivering it at the lowest possible cost, and making it available to every human being regardless of circumstance. Education is the lynchpin. If we just keep getting less intelligent, less capable of critical thinking, and less

prepared for the world ahead, how are we going to shape our society into a better world? The flaw in education over the last 60 or 70 years has been pretty much motivated toward economic productivity - back to the single measure.

We completely overlook how humans are, how we think, how we feel, fear, desire, or how humans learn and create. We are the most complicated and important variable in any part of any system that we are looking to improve, yet we ignore that variable. Technology shows up with all its fascinating opportunities, and the practitioners only see it as a cost-cutting tool and implement it that way. They fail to see how technology works with humans and how humans learn best.

We have seen a huge pendulum swing from analog to all digital, which hasn't really worked, in the sense that people have not engaged fully with it. And now we are seeing that pendulum swing back to the middle because that is probably where it works best. You have the benefit from the efficiencies of technology, but you don't ignore the realities of our humanity and how people want to learn. People learn best from people, so the future of education needs to be hybrid.

THE AGE OF DECADENCE

The more educated we become, the less likely we are to be intellectually lazy, and that could ultimately save humanity. Sir John Bagot Glubb wrote a paper in 1976 called 'The Fate of Empires and Search for Survival', where he studied empires and characterized six ages.

The pioneer age is followed by the age of conquest, followed by the age of commerce, then the age of affluence, then intellect, and finally, the age of decadence. He makes a clear and impassioned argument that every empire, from the beginning, follows the exact same arc and ends up in the age of decadence, which is a precursor to either demise or irreconcilable decline. Is this avoidable? Well, history tells us, unfortunately, no.

There have been hundreds and hundreds of major metropolises around the world, not just in Europe and Asia, that were thriving, bustling metropolises that just ended up disappearing. Market conditions, changes in technology, and geographic values are all attributable to the demise of one entity or another, but more than anything, I would argue that intellectual laziness is what really kills entities, countries, or companies. It's this arrogant, sense of entitlement, risk aversion attitude. America is deep in the age of decadence, characterized by its reverence towards sports personalities and celebrities over intellectuals, scientists, and professionals. Compare the pay of a footballer with that of a teacher - who do we value more?

In the US, we are also holding onto the past. Instead of creating a 21st Century American dream, half of our country wants to go backward. Donald Trump uses the slogan 'Make America Great Again', but it has nothing to do with progress. It's about reverting to where we were 50 or 60 years ago when white supremacy was alive and well. It's still pretty much alive and well, even today, but back then, it was in its heyday. So if we believe Glubb, unless we act and reset our intentions, we are heading for the demise or irreconcilable decline of America as we know it.

THE HUMAN REVOLUTION

I have been considering forming an organization called 'The Human Revolution'. It would be designed to be an aggregator of all the different individuals and institutions around the world who are realizing that in order to survive and thrive, we must do a better job of stewarding technology, capitalism, and, frankly, ourselves.

For example, the unleashing of technology, without stewardship, is the unleashing of the beast. Just like we unleash the capitalist beast. I reiterate, I'm not anti-capitalism or anti-technology, but I do think they require more active stewardship. By unleashing technology, we have changed the nature of the day, of the week, of the month - of life! We have found ourselves in a place where we can be so economically productive by transacting more. We can do it 24/7 because there is now no beginning or end to the working day, and that has yielded profound economic productivity around the world. On the other hand, the unintended consequence is having no space or even license to actually think.

So stewarding technology, capitalism, and ourselves means we need to adopt an increasing understanding of our behavior within this critical capacity. If you look at marriages that fail, it's not necessarily because people fall out of love, but because of a lack of understanding. So people need to wake up and reflect more. They need to begin to care more about understanding themselves and their loved ones. They need to care more about understanding strangers without bias or judgment. The more we understand ourselves, the more chance we will be able to mitigate unintended negative consequences, and then we will be able to realize the greatest potential for our species.

> "People need to wake up and reflect more, they need to begin to care more about understanding themselves, about understanding their loved ones. They need to care more about understanding strangers, without bias or judgment."

To see more on
Christopher Colbert

JOSH CHAN

CEO & Co-Founder at Halo AR

Originally, Josh's chosen vocation was teaching and after obtaining a degree in Human Biology, he went on to study for an MA in Education to become a science teacher. Yet whilst his career journey may have started in the classroom, it quickly pivoted into the world of technology and entrepreneurship.

Josh is the co-founder of LightUp, an e-learning provider which specializes in harnessing augmented reality for learners. His passion for teaching had never left him, and although he had withdrawn from the physical classroom, Josh remained committed to the virtual one and engaging students like never before.

His training in education and teaching practice proved to be an asset, and gave him a head start in the process of creating learning tools for students. The startup focused on producing realistic virtual science labs and 3D simulations accessible from anywhere via a digital device like a smartphone. With imaginative apps such as Animal Safari, Solar System, Bridge Builder and

Globe, the world becomes more easily accessible. It must have been a science teacher's dream to be able to captivate young minds with such visual stimulation. The Sugar app, for instance, uses a barcode which displays the amount of sugar in foods as visual representations of sugar cubes or donuts. The power of the image is at the heart of what Josh does and he declares it to be the most 'dangerous' 'immersive' and 'breathtaking' STEM (Science, Technology, Engineering, Math) learning experience within reach.

A natural progression from this concept is Halo AR (Augmented Reality). Its remit is to build global learning layers powered by augmented reality, expanding to a wider community, but still remaining within an educational framework. Museums, design houses, publishers and educational facilities can all benefit from supplementary videos and holograms to spark imaginations and bring learning to life.

Josh in his own words...

FROM TEACHING TO TECH

They say one step at a time, and that's what I did. I just followed my passion. I did not imagine I would become an entrepreneur or someone working in technology, I always wanted to be a teacher. I suppose I am one of a few teachers that ended up in entrepreneurship, but my educational experience has actually been a big advantage as I have been able to bring a different perspective to the process.

It started with just an amazingly simple app that lets anybody take a picture and then put something digital out into the real world. But as we are now accessing technology in new ways, innovations, like AR are going to change almost every aspect of our life. Imagine going around the world, being able to see specific information, where, and when you want to see it.

> "As we are now accessing technology in new ways, innovations, like AR are going to change almost every aspect of our life. Imagine going around the world, being able to see specific information, where, and when you want to see it."

As a company, we want to focus on the area which people find most meaningful, but with my educator hat on, I want to help people to learn about the world. That would, of course, include schools and classrooms, but other learning environments as well. Learning doesn't stop outside the classroom, if you go to a museum, you're learning, if you go to a workplace training session, you're learning, if you're simply reading a book at home, chances are, you're learning. There are so many ways that we are learning about things, and we don't even realize it.

To this extent, we are very much focused on going directly to teachers, as opposed to tech savvy Silicon Valley people, which can have its own set of obstacles. In most cases our AR system will be the users' first introduction to the technology. If people are unfamiliar with, and don't understand what we do, then they're not going to understand our product, therefore, we have had to create a process to get people to start to understand AR.

A CURIOSITY FULFILLMENT TOOL

I am happy to see that we've had people use Halo AR in all 50 of the American states, and it's hugely different making a product for the Bay Area, or Silicon Valley to somewhere in the Midwest, or a small town. We have users from primary to University, in many disciplines; art, science, history, and languages. Every subject under the sun has found a way to use our app. That's what I find pretty amazing. We provided an open-ended tool that didn't really have a lot of structure or requirements. And then people have really taken that and combined it with their creativity to apply it to everything.

We are focused on entertaining, educating and engaging with people, rather than purely creating something that is for fun. From my background as a teacher, and since college I have always had this strong belief that the greatest time and the greatest opportunity we have as adults to really make an impact is by working on technology that grows and develops with, and for the next generation. They are impressionable, and malleable and it's really a time when great good can be done, or great harm too. Being able to create technology that

"Being able to create technology that can empower people and create a positive experience is a privilege and a responsibility we take very seriously."

can empower people and create a positive experience is a privilege and a responsibility we take very seriously.

THE FUTURE IS AR

As a classroom practitioner I used a lot of resources which were perhaps outdated and simply not fit for purpose. For example, we were using the same textbooks in the science lab for decades. It was difficult at times to get the students engaged. My hope is that Augmented Reality brings the specific information you actually need, physically to where you need it. So that when a student is stuck, AR could potentially answer that question for the student.

Everything is becoming more personalized now, including education, and AR could be a personalized answer. It has the potential to be more engaging, more interactive, and more immersive. We also need to explore the potential technology has for speeding up the learning process in comparison with traditional learning methods. Right now, we're in a great position because smartphones and tablets have become so capable that we can power what we want to make, which was not possible even a few short years ago. Looking forward, we're extremely excited about the Metaverse.

Famously, Facebook changed their name to Meta. Apple is a bit of a dark horse, but there is a strong understanding that they are about to enter the AR space. As devices make it easier to access augmented reality, we will begin to see important changes, one of the biggest will probably be the way gestures

and expressions are virtually controlled. There's a group at Stanford working on a contact lens right now that's going to use augmented reality. As AR becomes more developed and widely accessible, it's impossible not to fantasize about its endless possibilities.

TECHNOLOGY IS MOVING FAST

We are going to see some fast changes within technology in the next 5-10 years. People forget that the iPhone came out in 2007, and then, even though it was a hit, it was still quite a niche product, nothing like the success that it became years later. They steadily improved it year after year, so the technology in the iPhone took leaps that brought it to where it is today.

The biggest things that are happening now is that Microsoft, and Meta / Facebook, have been running these giant chat applications, but they're clearly focusing now on virtual reality. I'm really excited about the potential, where you can be in your own office and bring a model for a new product or an architectural rendering, into this future version of zoom. We would love to be an enabler for that, where you could bring up that model and see it on the table in front of you. Even though the Metaverse isn't a prime focus for us today, we are building in that direction, and who knows what could happen in terms of future collaborations.

EDUCATION IS KEY

A few decades ago, devices were large and heavy and fixed to a desk, costing $1000s each to buy. The price point created a slower diffusion of technology. However, 15 years ago, the world was introduced to smartphone technology with the iPhone, and then more strongly with Android, and all of a sudden, adoption rates skyrocketed.

We now basically have two platforms, and it's very hard to support two platforms simultaneously. Like many companies, initially, we only built our tech for the iPhone, simply because that's what we all use. But we have been conscious to take that extra bit of labor to support Android, mainly because, around the world it's the number one operating system which allows us to get this worldwide usage, thus advancing the use of our product globally.

Since our platforms support Android, our hope for the future is that it can go some way in being impactful to the process of education on a global scale. For a number of diverse reasons, education in many countries is often denied to people. Obviously, basic needs such as food, water and shelter are natural priorities, but education is the missing piece of the puzzle. If you're living in a developing country, then education is what gets you learning about the skills and the knowledge you need to bring yourself to a better place.

Even in developed countries, when we consider the rise of AI and automation, we need this deep learning to get ahead of this disruption. Because if we are doing today what robots will be doing tomorrow, we need to be educated. If we can really transform how people learn, we have the potential to make this global impact and leap people and problems of today forward into a better tomorrow.

"If we can really transform how people learn, we have the potential to make this global impact and leap people and problems of today forward into a better tomorrow."

To see more on
Josh Chan

CULTIVATE RESILIENCE AND ADAPTABILITY

Nurture the ability to bounce back and adjust to changes. By viewing change as an opportunity, we can pave new paths, innovate, and flourish. In this unpredictable and ever-changing world, the ability to adapt and bounce back - resilience - becomes a pivotal factor for success. Resilience and adaptability don't merely keep us afloat during high tides, but also allow us to seize the underlying opportunities in the face of adversity.

"The oak fought the wind and was broken, the willow bent when it must and survived."

Robert Jordan

NATIONAL COUNTRY PROGRAMS

South Korea's rapid response to COVID-19, pivoting from an early outbreak to becoming a global exemplar, demonstrates national resilience and adaptability. Their robust testing, tracing, and quarantining strategies have paved the way for other nations.

CORPORATES

In response to the global pandemic, Toyota Motors promptly adjusted its manufacturing line to produce ventilators and masks. This resilience and adaptability to meet societal needs to demonstrate Toyota's commitment to making a difference, even in crisis situations.

NEW VENTURES AND STARTUPS

Slack, a business communication platform, saw a massive increase in users during the pandemic as companies shifted to remote work. Rather than buckling under pressure, Slack adapted to handle the increased demand, reinforcing the importance of resilience in a startup's growth.

LOCAL COMMUNITY CHANGE

The city of Detroit, once declared bankrupt, showcases resilience and adaptability as it reemerges as a hub for art, culture, and urban farming, demonstrating the power of community recovery.

INDIVIDUAL PERSONAL

Nick Vujicic, born without limbs, overcame immense personal challenges to become a world-renowned motivational speaker. His journey epitomizes resilience and adaptability, inspiring millions to overcome their personal barriers.

Resilience and adaptability are not inherited traits, but skills to be nurtured and developed. We can train ourselves to be flexible, to embrace change and turn it into opportunities. In doing so, we can pave new paths, innovate, and flourish, even amidst turbulence.

SIMON ALEXANDER ONG

Award Winning Life & Executive Coach
Keynote Speaker and Author of Energize

Some may think there is a huge jump from earning an Economics degree and working in finance to becoming a qualified life and executive coach. However, for Simon Ong, there are similarities in these disciplines. Both require analytical and problem-solving skills; both entail seeing patterns and detail and the strong ability to interpret complex information into simple language.

Essentially, Simon mentors people to become better versions of themselves by analyzing what they are doing, what they are not doing, and what they should be doing to achieve success. And his approach obviously works, as he has been hired by giants such as Microsoft, Barclays and Virgin to share his strategic methods in the corporate arena.

He has been featured in a number of publications and has recently penned his first book titled Energise, where he introduces the reader to the art and science of energy management. Although his life now is far away from the financial banking world, he still enjoys investing in financial markets and young start-ups. His other interests include magic, not just watching it but practicing close-up magic too. He also enjoys world cinema and keeping fit with Karate, Tae Kwon Do, and Wing Chun.

Simon in his own words...

The key thing I bring to an event like 'The Start-up Show' is my experience and the wisdom I've accumulated making the transition from being an employee to becoming an entrepreneur. Many attending will be aspiring entrepreneurs, people who are commonly doing things they don't regard as fulfilling and have this desire deep within them to do something more.

Although they know there is something more they want to do, they don't yet have the courage to do it. Being able to hear from myself and other speakers will hopefully not only inspire them but will become the catalyst they need to embark on that journey.

FROM BANKER TO COACH

I came from a stereotypical Asian household where it was drilled into you from a very young age that you had to be a banker, doctor, lawyer, or accountant. The definitions of success for me were very limited. After graduating with a Degree in Economics, I got a job in Canary Wharf, London. I was very excited at the time. It was my first job, and I remember telling my dad that I would work hard to get promoted.

This was a year before the global financial crisis in 2008. And just to make things a little more interesting, the company that I started with was Lehman Brothers, which later collapsed into administration. Although I managed to get another job, I was essentially in and out of work for nearly ten years.

Even though I worked in finance during the day, my spare time was spent exploring my curiosity for entrepreneurship.

> "I came from a very stereotypical Asian household where it was very much drilled into you from a very young age that you had to be a banker, doctor, lawyer, or an accountant."

> "As soon as we can detach ourselves from the outcome and focus on what is in our control, focus on what we can do and live in the present, we become consistent, because the goal becomes process based instead of outcome based."

It eventually came to me that my destiny would always be outside of my control as long as I worked for someone else. I started reading books, attending seminars, and surrounding myself with mentors, coaches, and guides. All this led me to what I now do today.

My wife mentioned an advert that she came across, about a two-day seminar about the coaching industry. I had always enjoyed helping other people, but I just considered it as nothing more than a hobby. However, my curiosity was sparked, and the event was free so I had nothing to lose apart from my time. By the end of the two days, I had signed up for the whole course. And, after two and half years, I graduated and qualified as a coach.

Once I started working, I found that I was pretty good at it, and I was invited by one of my clients to speak at a leadership seminar. This led to more paid public speaking events, and things just started to overlap and layer.

FOCUS ON THE PROCESS AND NOT THE OUTCOME

Typical clients I have worked with have been corporate executives, entrepreneurs, TV presenters, Michelin star chefs, and some celebrities. The process with these individuals is not really about what they should be doing but what habits stop them from making progress. Often, success can change who we are, and the secret lies in maintaining who you are despite your success. When somebody achieves fame, money, or unimaginable success, they can lose who they are.

Also, one of the things we don't appreciate is that with each level of success, most people's level of insecurity increases. For example, it's relatively straightforward when Michelin-star chefs work to get their first star; they can take risks. However, once they obtain their first Michelin star, they then have a certain level of pressure to get the second one. They have more to lose.

Because few people are ever prepared for that next stage in their careers, it's profoundly beneficial for them to be able to have a space where they can share and openly discuss what is going on.

Many of us attach our wellbeing to an outcome, and when this happens, we cease to become in control. We are giving up how we feel to something that is outside of our control. As soon as we can detach ourselves from the outcome and focus on what is within our control, focus on what we can do, and live in the present, we become consistent because the goal becomes process-based instead of outcome-based.

If you look at the world of sports, it may be easy to win your first trophy. But it is hard to defend and win that trophy year after year. Manchester United during the 90s, Roger Federer and Tiger Woods are all seen as legends because they were able to remain consistent over a number of years, perhaps because they were constantly focusing on the process and not the outcome.

To give an example, if you had a goal of becoming a bestselling author, you would focus on the *process* and not the *outcome*. You would write for 30 minutes every day, which is far easier to control than becoming a bestselling author. Instead of channeling your energy into the things that you can't control, which can paralyze you, you are focusing on what you can control, which energizes you and compels you to take action.

HEAD TO HEART

The longest journey that we make as humans is moving our interests from our heads to our hearts. Spirituality is very important. When most people look at energy, they only focus on the physical elements. We tend to neglect the mental, emotional, and spiritual, which are equally as important. My book, *Energise*, touches on four energy aspects: physical, mental, emotional, and spiritual.

You become low on spiritual energy when you are not doing the things that make you feel alive or going against the things that come naturally to you. You are high on spiritual energy when you have a connection to something bigger than yourself, something that makes you feel alive. What I've observed in society is that many people are exhausted, not because they are physically doing too much, but because they're doing too little of the things that make them feel alive.

Spirituality plays a big part in understanding who we are, because to understand who we are is the beginning of true wisdom. To have faith in a higher power is important. Whatever the world throws your way, there is always something that you can take from it, however small. Pronoia is the opposite of paranoia. It's where you believe that the universe is conspiring in your favor and that life is working for you, not against you. That way of looking at the world is far more productive.

I have touched on the spiritual side of energy, but there remains the obvious

> **"Thomas Edison would go fishing every day but without any bait so that no one, not even the fish, would disturb him. It was in those moments that he would have creative breakthroughs, insight, and sparks of wisdom."**

one, and that is physical energy. Prioritizing time for yourself is important. This may sound like pretty basic stuff, but if you look at ambitious leaders, people who want to achieve a lot in their life, slowing down and having time to re-energize becomes an issue. How often are they blocking out time in the calendar? That's usually the first place I start. How much sleep do they get? How often are they moving their body? Are they as quick to make time for themselves as they are in accepting business invitations? Because until they have something like that in place, there is not really much point in talking about the other areas.

I can say to them "yes, you need to do this, you need to do that," but if their calendar is already busy and overpacked, they won't have time to do any of it. We all need to allow ourselves space. Where there is space, energy can flow into it. All of us crave creativity, innovation and insight, but the irony is we don't give ourselves time for those things to come to us. Silence is far from empty. In fact, it's full of answers.

Thomas Edison would go fishing every day but without any bait so that no one, not even the fish, would disturb him. It was in those moments that he would have creative breakthroughs, insight, and sparks of wisdom. There is real value in doing nothing. Isaac Newton for example, sat under a tree doing nothing until an apple fell on his head, and he discovered gravity. It is in those moments of disconnect that we allow ourselves to connect to our true self.

EDUCATION AND CHANGING THE CURRICULUM

I have done talks at secondary schools and have worked with some teachers who are responsible for the rollout of programs and what goes into curriculums. I can see a lot of areas where improvements could be made. For example, making time during the school day for meditation and mindfulness can achieve impressive results. Visitacion Valley High School in San Francisco embraced quiet time for one year, and the school went from the bottom third to the top third of schools ranked in the city.

Money management is also a very important skill, as well as

public speaking and communication. I am championing these real-world skills. In a world in which you can go on to Google, Alexa or now, chatGPT and ask a question and get the answer back in seconds. What's the purpose of memorizing facts and figures?

The greatest impact that the internet has had is that it has leveled the playing field. No matter if you are a young child or an old retiree, it allows any of us to build a business and to share our knowledge. And to have an impact, whatever age you are, there have been 6-year-olds who are making millions of dollars on YouTube, reviewing toys. There are 95-year-olds launching apps on app stores. Far better to teach our children and the next generation the skills that will help them in the outside world now. The educational system as it is, is just not fit for the world that we live in today.

SURFING THE WAVE

This world is changing at a rapid pace, and those who can adapt are going to be the ones who learn to surf this wave. In fact, the analogy connected to adaptability is that we've got to be better surfers. Waves will always come, introducing new trends and changing industries, but if we learn to surf these waves, we become adaptable. Whatever the world throws your way, you will be able to adapt and come back stronger.

When I published my book, I looked at ways of getting people's attention. For example, we partnered with the Conrad Hotel, where they created an 'Energised Cocktail' to mark the launch of the book. For one month, anyone who ordered the cocktail would have it presented to them on a copy of my book. We also partnered with a web-free educational platform to put together one of the world's first book launches in the metaverse. We surfed the waves in order to reach new audiences because as the world becomes more distracted, attention is becoming more important.

MY LEAPFROG MOMENT AND SUGGESTION TO THE WORLD

The biggest leapfrog is the realization and appreciation that you only have one life.

There is a great Aristotle quote that goes: You have two lives. That second life begins the very moment you understand you only have one.

In April 2020, I became a father for the very first time. It was during lockdown and I was only allowed in the ward for an hour after the birth. I was holding my newborn daughter in my arms, and I remembered something very powerful, that we are all miracles. The fact that we are born is a miracle event in itself. The chances of me meeting my wife, the chances that we could have a child, and the chances of us having this particular child is just a miracle.

Many of us wish we would win the National Lottery, that we would win the jackpot. But we already have won the greatest lottery ticket there is… The lottery of life.

The question is, what are you going to do with that winning ticket of yours?

"If we can really transform how people learn, we have the potential to make this global impact and leap people and problems of today forward into a better tomorrow."

To see more on
Simon Alexander Ong

EMBODY A NORTH STAR MINDSET

Cultivate a mindset that is unwavering and resolute in its direction and purpose, akin to the constant North Star. This mentality helps maintain focus and determination on the leapfrogging journey, regardless of the challenges encountered. In our quest for leapfrogging, amidst the hustle and bustle of innovation, there lies a profound insight often left unexplored—the North Star Mindset. This mindset calls for a purpose that stands unwavering, a vision that is clear and steadfast, akin to the constant North Star. It is a mindset that, despite the ebbs and flows of change, stays resolute in its direction and purpose.

"We need to find the compass in ourselves. We need to have the guts and the courage to confront everything we are, everything we do, and have the compass guide us to our true north."

William Deresiewicz

NATIONAL COUNTRY PROGRAMS

Bhutan, with its North Star of Gross National Happiness, has focused on holistic development and wellbeing over conventional economic growth. Despite economic pressures, Bhutan has stood firm on its values, reflecting the power of a North Star Mindset.

CORPORATES

Apple Inc., guided by its North Star of making great products that enrich people's lives, has revolutionized the tech industry. Despite various challenges, Apple has remained focused on its vision, thus transforming the face of personal technology.

NEW VENTURES AND STARTUPS

Tesla Motors, with a clear vision of accelerating the world's transition to sustainable energy, has been unwavering in its approach, illustrating how a firm North Star can drive transformation.

LOCAL COMMUNITY CHANGE

The city of Curitiba in Brazil has held firm to its vision of urban sustainability, becoming a global model for innovative urban planning. Despite resource constraints, they've created a well-functioning city, proving the power of a North Star.

INDIVIDUAL PERSONAL

Malala Yousafzai, the youngest Nobel laureate, embodies a North Star Mindset with her unwavering commitment to girls' education. Her dedication, despite the dangers she faced, is a testament to the strength of a clear and determined purpose.

Just as the North Star guides travelers, our goals and purpose should be the unwavering constants guiding our actions. Holding on to our North Star, we can navigate the tumultuous sea of change and innovation without losing our path. The North Star Mindset helps maintain focus, providing the willpower to overcome obstacles and enabling leapfrogging.

CHRIS BROWNE

CEO/Co-Founder KIT London

If you were to stumble across Chris Browne and his impressive LinkedIn page, under the section Education, you would read "Hah! None," a humorous quip that can only be delivered by a man who's reached the very top of his game. As a retail enthusiast, consultant, and mentor, Chris opened the first Ted Baker store in 1988, growing the brand to a value of £1.6 billion. He can afford a bit of tongue-in-cheek.

Interestingly, his approach to business has been shaped by observing his early mentors and choosing to do things differently. His eagerness to avoid emulating his father's temper taught him to develop patience and an even-keeled management style. At the same time, bullying tactics by his area manager encouraged a more polite, approachable, and humorous attitude. But, above all, his mother's enduring optimism in the face of adversity reminds him always to stay positive and enthused.

Now, with more than 40 years of experience in retail, it is clear that the industry still excites Chris. He is currently a director and co-founder of KIT LONDON, a new brand in apparel "capable of anything." Out of the office, there are many exciting aspects to the man. Erudite, knowledgeable, and eclectic in his passions, Chris completely contradicts the maxim about getting good grades. A keen gardener and apiarist, he talks about 'overwintered hives' and decanting '30 lbs of honey' with the modesty of a seasoned beekeeper. He also says he is "The most ridiculous bookworm you'll ever meet," often having 7 or 8 books on the go at once. He keeps tropical fish and is a self-proclaimed racquet sports devotee, "If you name a racquet sport, I probably play it." For a man in his early 60s, he is strikingly youthful and swears by magnesium supplements for his exuberant spirit.

> **"Paying mere lip service to sustainability is no longer enough."**

Chris in his own words...

RETAIL IS THERAPY

From a young age, I have been particularly enthusiastic about the world of commerce and retail, and I think we will see many changes in how we produce, buy, and sell. Paying mere lip service to sustainability is no longer enough, and I hope we will revert to a time when nations and towns go back to manufacturing. A combination of old-fashioned production with new tech in fashion is necessary - we need to bring back meaningful processes rather than just focusing on mindless selling.

My first job was at the age of 12. I worked at a newsagent early in the morning, marking up the papers to be delivered. I also sold sweets and chocolates and noticed how natural I was at selling. I enjoyed the banter and the back-and-forth before the sale. On Saturdays, I worked at a tropical fish store and loved the activity of selling. The trickier the customer, the better - I enjoyed the challenge. The psychology of buying and selling is fascinating; every customer who walks into the shop brings in a different persona or a different set of characteristics, and you can tailor your approach to that individual customer. It's interesting that, through sheer effort, you can persuade someone to buy something. How the product is displayed, how you've talked about it, how you've negated any objections, or even how you've entertained them can be why they decide to purchase.

LEAPFROGGING

I have learned two essential things in retail: keep your anger under wraps and believe something can always come along and change the trajectory. At Ted Baker, our trajectory changed dramatically when we trialed a new type of fabric, which customers picked up on quickly. It was the mid 90's, and we knew the product had the potential to corner the market and take the brand to another level. We obtained more fabric in the coming weeks, increased productivity, and doubled turnover. It was our leapfrog moment. One year later, every store was doing twice the previous year's turnover, and the secret to our success was knowing how to build on that.

Another leapfrog moment came when we launched two stores in America, almost simultaneously, one in San Jose and one in Miami. The store in San Jose was based in a new shopping center that burned down due to an arson attack. Our opening had been delayed, and I was asked to give an interview for what I believed to be a local newscaster. I incorporated some London cockney rhyming slang during the interview and returned to work. A few hours later, my colleague rang me to say that I had just been on CBS News with an audience of 40 million! Promoting Ted Baker's arrival to so many people was a massive stroke of luck for the brand and helped move the trajectory upwards.

"The West seems blind to the world of technology and how it can enhance not just industry but wider society."

A PERSONAL LEAPFROG

Before Ted Baker, I worked in a shoe shop on King's Road in Chelsea. It was the place to go for fashion, and I served many celebrities in that store. I remember once when Princess Diana, who knew my name, entered the store and addressed me informally as "Chris." The fact that she knew me and cared for me was a very personal leapfrog moment. She used to come in a couple of times a month and just wanted to be treated like everyone else in the store. That was both an honor and a lesson in kindness that I will never forget. I applied it to my strategy from that moment on.

VISUAL TECH

I have worked with a number of companies that provide future tech solutions, and there's quite a lot of resistance and conceit when I approach businesses with these applications. They state that they have either seen the technology before, already understood it, or have a version of it. Having worked a lot in Asia, I find it astounding how far ahead China is in the way that they engage with technology. There, when companies have vast inventories of goods that often include over 150,000 items, it may take several hours to find one product. But, if you use the latest technology available, it can be done in the blink of an eye.

Using technology also affords you a greater understanding of social media algorithms and how you have to manipulate them. The general public perhaps doesn't appreciate just how sophisticated it is. Posting the right things at the right moment at the right time of the week is crucial to create the greatest impact. Again, there are systems and software out there that will show you how to do that.

In my experience, the West seems blind to the world of technology and how it can enhance not just industry but wider society. I think every organization should have a futurist embedded in it. It's one of my passions, and I think it's necessary if companies want to protect themselves against future failure. They should have a futurist who spends all of their time looking at the software opportunities, tracking any changes happening in the company's or the public's mood, buying habits, or needs.

FROM SCIENCE FICTION TO FACT

Although I am an advocate for using all the tech we can, I would also like a return to more locally produced goods that provide meaning and value to the people of that area. Small, unique places still allow visitors to take a little part of it home with them, but with increased global mass production, they're becoming increasingly rare. I went to a market in Florence where everything was imported from China. What's the point of going to Ponte Vecchio and not being able to buy something unique to that area?

While I would welcome a return to more local commercial practice, I also believe the future is 'liquid,' and soon you'll be able to receive goods in a dried or liquid form that will go into a processing unit in your own kitchen; if you wanted a pizza, you could put the 'formula' into the machine, press the right buttons, and have all your favorite toppings and the desired crust. The burger industry is investing in a similar technology for burger production. The biggest threat to their industry is the environmental process of raising, killing, and transporting cattle. If they become able to transport only the essential constituents instead, it will be cheaper and more manageable, plus the food can be made to the customer's exact requirements.

I also think augmented humans will become significant in the near future. At some point, we will no longer use a phone; our ears will work as receivers, and our lips will have speakers implanted. Augmented contact lenses would mean that you could project messages in front of you or be guided through unfamiliar city streets with just a blink of an eye. The technology will expand, and it's a revolution that is coming quickly.

Many potential future things that sound like science fiction are happening but will soon become our normality. The means of travel will also change. Once we have learned how to go above the stratosphere economically, we will be able to wait for the Earth to turn, then come back down twenty minutes later and be in a different part of the world.

Aging will be a thing of the past. We will be able to choose an age and then enhance it. I would choose to be 40 years old but with better leg muscles than the average man of that age. I know Elon Musk is working on neuro-link technology. Effectively, you'd be able to tell your brain to 'think in German,' and you would do so.

Beyond all the technological advancement and exponential change, I'd also like to see a global leapfrog return to the hippy concept of "peace and love." It may sound cliche, but anger on a global scale is pandemic-level, whether it's about gender, pronouns, race, or even road rage. Why not just default to positivity? Why not default to happiness and enjoy life? We need a "Choose happiness" movement, and I think people would be amazed by the impact a positive mindset can have.

ENHANCEMENTS

I read a book called Miracle of Magnesium by Carolyn Dean and found that the earth has been depleted of magnesium because of all the fertilizers we use. If it's not in the ground, it's certainly not in our food. It's not a conspiracy theory either; you can measure a stalk of broccoli or a banana to gauge the low magnesium levels.

I started taking magnesium for entirely different reasons. I played many sports, so I was sweating a lot and thought

"Soon, you'll be able to receive goods in a dried or liquid form that will go into a processing unit in your own kitchen."

taking supplements would be a good idea. I was advised by a doctor that I needed more potassium and magnesium in my system, and I started there. Now, 40 years later, I have good skin and no gray hair. I look younger than my age and am physically still very fit and strong.

I am evangelical in my attitude to taking supplements. The advances in supplementation are going to shock people. There are now, already, new neural-affecting pills that will literally make your brain razor-sharp. If you can take something that makes you sharper, faster, wiser, healthier, or even sleep better, then why not?

BOOKS TO CHANGE YOUR LIFE

I am a voracious reader, and one book I recommend to everyone is *Illusions* by Richard Bach. I met the author, and he's an amazing character. It's a short, allegorical book about mentorship - it's fundamentally about making your dreams a reality, whatever they might be. It's a fantastic read.

I would also recommend *WHIM* by Luke Rhinehart. It's about a 'magical' Indian boy sent to Earth to find the 'Ultimate Truth." I definitely identify with the main character as someone who doesn't do things just because that's how everyone else does them. You should follow, or plow, your own furrow - that's my advice for anyone.

Lastly, the book, *You: The Owner's Manual* by Mehmet C Oz MD and Michael F Roizen MD, explains how your body works, how to make it work better, and how to take care of it. It's written like a car manual but for the human body. It's a fun and informative read.

> "Errors come in because you make decisions based on growth rather than what's right for the health of the business."

MENTORSHIP

A while ago, I invested in a company called Jelly Drops. It's a company creating hydrating sweets that are 95% water and a highly beneficial product for the elderly, particularly those with dementia who can forget to drink fluids. I got involved in the company because I thought it was a great idea, and I now advise and mentor the principal founder, Lewis Holtby. In many parts of the world, elderly care is appalling, particularly in the UK. If we can improve older adults' lives, we can learn from them and document their stories for future generations.

I happily conduct advisory and mentoring work. I enjoy doing it, and I don't charge. It is my way of giving back. Having had a long and successful commercial career, I feel that I can give advice, even if it is just generic thoughts and ideas around a specific question or problem.

TAKE TIME TO THINK!

I advise small companies to slow down. There is this obsession with getting the business to scale and exit fast for a profit. In my opinion, errors come in because you make decisions based on growth rather than what's right for the health of the business.

At Ted Baker, we did things in a very cautious, very solid way. I advise companies to slow down, look at the technology out there, and see how it can work for them. Think about incorporating the tech, but don't overspend on it. If you get it right, people will come. You don't have to run that fast, do what's right for you as individuals and do what's right for other people down the chain of the business. Finally, ensure you have a succession plan because you won't want to do it forever.

> "There are already new neural-affecting pills that will literally make your brain razor-sharp."

To see more on
Chris Browne

MR RANGASWAMI

Founder at Indiaspora
CEF & Sand Hill Group

A community builder, philanthropist, entrepreneur, eco-strategist, and software executive investor, MR (pronounced M.R and not Mister) Rangaswami is undoubtedly a multifaceted man, who only really wants to be known as "a guy who is helpful." A very humble wish for a man who arrived in the USA as a university student with only $8 in his pocket.

He is listed in the Forbes Midas 100 list of most successful investors. He has been profiled in two books. In 2013, his network forum Indiaspora hosted the first Indian American Ball for the President of the USA, with a crowd of 1,200 Indian Americans joining politicians and policymakers in celebrating the accomplishments of the Indian community in America.

Highlighting a few areas that hold MR's interest, apart from the most obvious one, which is undoubtedly philanthropy. He is an inspirational speaker who, unusually, does not command a fee for sharing his knowledge and expertise with the audience and prefers a donation to go directly to a non-profit organization. His speaking topics have ranged from Entrepreneurship and Risk, On Baby Boomers, and Giving Back and Technology Driving Sustainability in Large Corporates.

MR is now based in San Francisco, CA, where he lives with his family. He relaxes by watching sports, walking, drinking good wine, and eating equally good vegetarian food. Curiously, he is an avid Australian football fan, something that no one else in the US watches, perhaps flagging an indication of his individual outlook.

"It's not about how great we are doing, but how much better we can do."

MR Rangaswami in his own words...

NETWORKING FOR GOOD

When you look at successful communities, you need to look at the organizer, the founder, the initial instigator of the community. There has to be a level of authenticity, a pure value of the greater good of the community itself. And they need to be very transparent; they shouldn't have their own personal, hidden agendas, like getting rich or famous.

I have spent 40 years in my career and have started three networks. One is the enterprise CEO network, consisting of 100 CEOs in the software industry. The other is the Corporate Eco Forum (CEF), which comprises 75 of the world's largest corporations and their Chief Sustainability Officers. The third one is the Indiaspora, an organization that unites the Indian diaspora, transforming its success into meaningful impact. These are all very separate and distinct networks, but one thing they have in common is the importance of shared values from day one.

When I started the networks, my agenda was the goodness of the community. It wasn't about me making money or gaining fame and fortune or any of that nonsense. Yes, there has got to be money made somehow, but if you don't go in from the start with a greater purpose, then the community rarely stays together, and they slowly disperse.

THE ENTERPRISE CEO NETWORK

I have learned from the tech network that it is best to lead with philanthropy. For example, when I started that network, I wanted the entire profits to be given to non-profit endeavors. I devised a business model that turned everything on its head because until then, every conference in the tech space was about the conference organizers making lots of money. From the start, it was all about us giving back, and I think it is a concept you need to build in any company. From that basis, great things can develop.

When the retreats began 25 years ago, everyone was selling enterprise software for thousands, even millions of dollars, which would be utilized over time. However, we've now seen this extraordinary shift in the industry to 'pay as you go.' Enterprise software evolved to 'software as a service,' now, instead of having that massive outlay, you pay small amounts each month. I think our group facilitated that change; it was a catalyst, and it transformed the way that the industry served its customers.

This concept of first doing good, which I started 25 years ago, still stands true today. Money is off the table, and it gives such a different feel to people coming into a retreat or a conference. It is all about sharing, giving, and learning, and not about money. To date, we have given over $2m to non-profit organizations, and the people who have come to our events have given even more; in fact, there is a 10:1 leverage factor in this process. Now we are looking at a total of around $20m shared out to non-profit organizations.

"When you start by having a greater purpose within an organization, and everyone agrees to it, then you can really leapfrog."

THE CORPORATE ECO FORUM

The Corporate Eco Forum consists of Chief Sustainability Officers who come together with the intent of tackling climate change. Again, it's not about how great *we* are doing but how much *better* we can do. The typical conferences on sustainability have companies boasting about how much they have achieved, but with the CEF, they say what *needs* to be achieved and how we can collectively do it. Again, it is this ethos of shared values, collaboration, and working together for a greater purpose.

When I started the Corporate Eco Forum 15 years ago, corporations were not talking about sustainability, net zero pledges, or the environmental social governance framework, all the things we have today. We were at the forefront, not because it was in fashion or trendy, but because we felt it was the right time to do it. You can't wait and do it next year. When the CEF was formed, it was new, and corporations were curious, and we used their curiosity to bring them together. And when you start by having a greater purpose within an organization, and everyone agrees to it, you can really leapfrog. When everyone has a shared value right from the start, gets together, agrees they should be doing something more extraordinary, thinking of a new solution, and thinking outside of the box, a lot starts to happen. It's all about mindset too.

INDIASPORA

Indiaspora is my third network, a diaspora leadership network. Again, it has been built to be a force for good. The Indian diaspora is 32 million people, the largest diaspora in the world, living outside of India. We make up only 1% of the US population but have 60 CEOs in the Fortune 500, that's 12%. In the US, there are 200,000 doctors of Indian origin, which means Indians make up 7% of all the doctors in the US. In IT, Indians take up 10% of the workforce. In academia, there are 20,000 Indian American professors. Those statistics dispel the myth that you have to be of a particular ethnicity to be successful. I think there are several reasons why Indians take up such a large percentage of these professions in the USA. One reason has to be down to the English

language. Having no language barrier must be an asset; I think that has been an advantage we have had over other ethnicities. Before the English language became prevalent in India, there were 22 languages spoken and 800 dialects, making it difficult for people to communicate. The use of the English language could be seen as a unifying factor and an asset for those Indians who moved to the US. Another reason why I think Indians take up a large percentage of the workforce in certain areas in America is because we value education. Education is number one in Indian culture. Indian parents want their kids to be doctors, lawyers, and computer scientists. It's just ingrained and has become inculcated in the community. I was an exception to the rule. I first became an accountant, then a lawyer, and then an MBA. They couldn't pigeonhole me. I wasn't one of those stereotypical Indian professionals. I was one of the few that came out of that rigid mindset.

THE FUTURE OF TECH IS AI

Having been in the technology industry for the past 40 years, I think the area that holds the most significant promise is artificial intelligence. We can tap into nothing more extraordinary over the next decade. The recent rollout of chat GPT, a chatbot that can interact conversationally, is the tip of the iceberg. Imagine what it's going to be like in 5-10 years. There could also be many more extraordinary things that could be done with AI in healthcare and education, etc. I think we are just starting to leverage it and monetize it, and if I am doing anything in the next ten years, it will be about harnessing the potential for AI.

THE FUTURE OF OUR PLANET / A LEAPFROG IDEA

We are now living in an existential crisis, and most of us see little of the massive impact of heavy rain, drought, or extreme weather. It comes and goes, and people tend to forget about it. How can we solve the climate crisis? I would like to see the same money and energy spent that we had during the .com bubble, which arose 20 years ago. $100b of private capital got thrown into crazy companies, and 99% of those failed, but from that came the internet - Google, Facebook, LinkedIn, Amazon, and Apple. If we do the same thing to solve climate change, throw private capital at the issue and see if anything develops which will ultimately solve the issue.

"Having been in the technology industry for the past 40 years, I think the area that holds the biggest promise is around artificial intelligence."

To see more on
MR Rangaswami

PROMOTE SUSTAINABILITY

Incorporate environmental, social, and economic sustainability into leapfrogging strategies. This approach ensures lasting benefits without compromising the wellbeing of future generations. In the heart of progressive leapfrogging, there is an insight that beckons our attention—Promoting Sustainability. As we navigate through the realms of advancement and progress, it is essential to ensure that our strategies and initiatives integrate the principles of environmental, social, and economic sustainability. This is the key to ensuring lasting benefits without compromising the wellbeing of our future generations.

"We do not inherit the earth from our ancestors, we borrow it from our children."

Native American Proverb

NATIONAL COUNTRY PROGRAMS

Denmark's commitment to renewable energy and sustainable living is commendable. As of 2020, more than half of the country's energy production comes from renewable sources, showing how national programs can embody sustainability.

CORPORATES

Unilever, with its Sustainable Living Plan, has committed to doubling the size of the business while reducing its environmental footprint and enhancing its positive social impact. This illustrates how corporations can prosper economically while promoting sustainability.

NEW VENTURES AND STARTUPS

Beyond Meat, a plant-based meat substitute producer, embodies sustainability by reducing the environmental impact associated with meat production. Its innovative product caters to growing consumer consciousness about the environment and animal welfare.

LOCAL COMMUNITY CHANGE

In Colombia, the city of Medellín transformed its transport infrastructure, incorporating cable cars into public transit, reducing emissions, and connecting underprivileged communities to the city center. It stands as a testament to how local initiatives can promote social and environmental sustainability.

INDIVIDUAL PERSONAL

Swedish activist Greta Thunberg has become a global icon for her stance on climate change. Her unwavering commitment to environmental sustainability has inspired millions, displaying the potential power of individual action.

Promoting sustainability is not merely an option—it's an obligation. As we leapfrog into the future, let us ensure that our steps are environmentally sound, socially responsible, and economically viable. By promoting sustainability, we build a world that respects and safeguards the legacy of our future generations.

DR. AKHTAR BADSHAH, PhD

Founder and Chief Catalyst
Catalytic Innovators Group

Author, artist, and successful entrepreneur Dr. Akhtar Badshah, PhD is effectively changing the discussion from 'passion' to 'purpose mindset.'

As a sharply focused humanitarian and internationally recognized expert on social impact, Akhtar has traveled extensively to meet with the poorest and most in need. This act of deep observation has allowed him to better understand how non-profit organizations can best use technology to affect lasting social change. Subsequently, he has created community programs made freely available on a global scale with the intention of helping others to help themselves.

A clever and contemplative individual with many strings to his bow, Akhtar has a Masters and Ph.D. in Architecture and Environmental Studies from MIT. He is also an accomplished abstract artist. Working with acrylic on canvas and layered plywood, his artwork is vibrant, emotive, and clearly influenced by his experiences in India.

His energy and 'purpose mindset' expands even further into the world of philanthropy. As the Senior Director of Microsoft Citizenship and Public Affairs, he led Microsoft's philanthropy program for ten years. He serves on the board of directors for several organizations and is the founder and Chief Catalyst of Catalytic Innovators Group (CIG), a consulting practice focused on accelerating social impact.

Akhtar in his own words...

CALAMITY AS A CATALYST

In the last two years since Covid first arrived, we have been going through an enormous transformation - our lives have been upended, and we are doing things that we never thought we would ever do.

> "We need to move away from the way we see the world to understanding the way other people see their world."

This is yet another example of the enormous capacity for humans to adapt and how resilient we are in the face of uncertainty, something that has been seen many times throughout documented history. But I wanted to challenge the existing mindset, the notion that growth is all we should be focused on. For a very long time, the focus in business has been on growth and passion, and I feel these two words to be incredibly selfish because they make everything about the individual or company and nothing else. Of course, both growth and passion are important. I wrote my book to reframe this. I wanted to know, why do we humans exist? Why do these corporations and organizations exist? A broader question of 'why?' and, the biggest of all, is 'what is your soul?' Purpose mindset is really about getting the deepest why's.

To be clear, purpose is the why. The mission, vision, and growth are only the how. People often say to me they want to be a CEO, and my first question is always, why? They rarely have a comprehensive answer. That all changes after creating a purpose statement. A light comes on. A eureka moment. We know it works, and not one of them is the same because everyone has a specific life purpose when they search inside. This is a personal way to 'leapfrog' in life.

Humanity, however, has shifted the narrative to a point where work is all we think about. We now 'live to work' rather than the other way around. Capitalism has become the root of society rather than only being the 'root' of business.

I believe purpose should be the basis of society, and in my book 'Purpose Mindset: How Microsoft Inspires Employees and Alumni to Change the World', I articulate a set of principles around purpose to assist in enabling people to move their focus from the 'me' to the 'we', and to serve the collective good.

For the last year, my company Catalytic Innovators Group has been conducting 'purpose mindset' workshops across the world, working with everyone from young students to CEOs of major companies and even governments. We have discovered that when you get people to focus on their strengths and values, and then craft a 'Purpose Statement,' they suddenly see the good in themselves and the wider world.

LEAPFROGGING

It is now my mission in life to ensure that everyone has an opportunity to craft their own purpose statement - and then live and take actions to achieve that written purpose.

When people define their purpose in this way, it enables them to leapfrog through life because, once a person knows and understands their true self, they can take giant steps forward. Not only in terms of their career but also in their relationships and every other aspect of their life.

"Life is not so much about who you want to be, it is actually about who you want to serve."

We have all, I am sure, spent way too much time focused on solving problems. I'm asking people to forget the problems and envision the future they want to live in.

Define your purpose, values, and strengths and apply them to yourself, your family, your community, and your work. Life is not so much about who you want to be, it is about who you want to serve.

EMPATHY & HUMANITY

We need to move away from the way we see the world to a new understanding; the way other people see their world. That is empathy.

I have always been a stickler for timekeeping. I did not like people arriving late into my office or classroom. However, my mindset was changed by one particular female student who came late to my four-hour Saturday morning class every time.

One day, I asked her why? She told me that she was a single mother and had to drive 60 minutes to come to class. She explained that "sometimes, there is traffic, sometimes, the babysitter arrives late, or the car is not starting."

Still, she came to class every time, participated, and did everything that I asked of her. She also asked me a question that changed my perspective, "why does it matter to you? How does it affect you if I am 30 minutes late?" A valid question and one that I had never previously considered. That young lady made me take stock and think again.

Learning to have humility can take many forms. I have spent many years visiting refugee camps and slums and, when asked, I have never refused to go, never said a space is too dirty or too risky. I have always gone to learn and help where I can. I always sit with people, eat the food, and drink the water I have been kindly offered by all those I met. If it made me sick, fine, it made me sick. It was always worth doing.

The biggest single life lesson I have learned was, in those moments, learning how to be human. It is what I believe drives innovation. It is how I have learned to be 'human-centered' in a very deep way, not in a superficial way, to take the time required to understand the humanity of every person and to treat them with dignity.

A SHIFT IN THINKING

I don't think of myself as an 'innovator'. I think the word is overused - I simply live my life.

When I attended MIT, I wanted to be an architect. But when I began teaching Islamic architecture and traveling the world, I started seeing humanity in a very different way. My thinking shifted, I was able to consider what people actually needed.

Did they need a building? Or did they need jobs? If they had jobs and money, they could surely build something for themselves. Why did they need me? That ability to shift my mind allowed me to move into different and exciting career paths.

Over the last four years, I have worked on things that I knew little or nothing about. I am not a philosopher. I'm not a sociologist. I am simply somebody who is walking this wonderful Earth in a very meaningful way. I make sure I am really observing and not just looking. And, through that act of observation, I can take my skills - my ability to speak, to write, and to paint - and share them with the world.

AN IDEA TO CHANGE THE WORLD

Every individual should have the confidence to say: 'This is who I am.' I believe sharing this message is the value I bring to the world, to my life, to my family, to my community, and to my work.

If all of us were able to do that, we would be in a much better place.

After I wrote 'Purpose Mindset', I started giving talks, but I was always thinking of different ways to impart the information. In one 40-minute interactive exercise, I asked my participants to share their strengths, values, and purpose, creating a situation in which they could discover themselves. It worked far better than I could have imagined! And, in a very structured form, that exercise became the product we created for organizations - a workshop that tells you who you are and enables you to learn the benefits of knowing yourself better than anybody else. It teaches you to forget about your weaknesses and talk about your strengths, your values, and your personal purpose.

That is a 'world-changing' idea. That is the change I want to see. It has to be led from behind so that others can take the concept and run with it, to come up with new ideas that allow it to evolve. Some will succeed; others will fail and personally, I befriend failure; I learn from it.

AKHTAR'S TAKEAWAY

Everyone has a purpose; they simply may not know what it truly is. They have not taken the time to dig deep into themselves for the 'why' before the 'how'. There is nothing intrinsically wrong with wanting a corporate title, or more money, simply that, with a fully defined personal purpose you are able to do things more effectively not only for personal benefit but also for societal benefit. You will act and speak differently. You will make different connections. You will improve society to the best of your ability. Leadership is about aligning skills on purpose. You can be the human that your soul, and the wider world, wishes it to be; on purpose.

To see more on
Dr. Akhtar Badshah PhD

Dr. Akhtar Badshah, PhD

The Art of Leapfrogging

SCOTT SPANN

Strategist & Creator of Emergent Impact™

From growing up working on ranches and fishing boats in South Texas where he was a cowboy, hunter, and fisherman, Scott Spann pivoted his destiny, exchanging his horse and fishing boat for a place at the table with some of the most influential and revolutionary leaders.

Inspired by his experiences with "business leaders trying to do the right thing in complex and competitive situations," Scott has had a diverse career, from consulting with Arthur Andersen & Co to launching the Texas office of The Nature Conservancy. He's worked with big beasts such as the US. Navy, Apple and HP to achieve results they thought were "impossible", but his true passion is to heal business, society and the Earth.

As an internationally competitive athlete, Scott has worked with Olympic athletes, doctors, and therapists, as a Rolfer and trauma developmental psychotherapist, to awaken the body's innate healing abilities. Until a little over a year ago, Scott lived an idyllic, minimalist life on a sailboat in Sausalito, California. Currently, he is based in Austin, Texas, where he has happily settled down near to friends and family.

Scott in his own words...

LEAPFROGGING BY SEEING THE WHOLE

"You need a 360-degree view of the 'whole'."

When we step back and begin to think about the 'whole' and what the 'whole' is trying to accomplish, it enables us to have an authentic, inclusive, and mutually beneficial conversation about the issues as an ecosystem. That ecosystem can be anything from a business or society, to a community or the Earth itself, but nevertheless, it needs to be seen as a 'whole' organism.

I'm on the board of an international organization that protects rivers and their communities, primarily by stopping dams. However, they have become so attached to stopping dams that they're seen as opposing what dams are actually there for; flood control, energy production, and reliable water supplies. They're not. So they're leapfrogging to a higher level of thought leadership by incorporating the needs of all stakeholders. They're taking a 360 degree view of the "whole" and executing on that.

Another example of how necessary it is to see the 'whole' comes from a project I worked on in Guatemala. Our job was to create alignment between diverse groups of people with different perspectives and ideologies. The situation was complicated and entailed building relationships with specific groups, including former guerrillas, the military, shamans, Catholic priests, economic ministers, and university students - 30 perspectives in all. There were oppositional forces among those stakeholders, and our aim was to develop a relationship between these groups for alignment to occur - a relationship via a shared reality.

When I interviewed a former guerrilla leader, his 'Hello' to me was "What is a rich white boy from San Francisco going to teach me about poverty and social injustice in Guatemala?" Of course, he was right. I knew nothing of those things. But I did know how to solve complex, multi-stakeholder problems like the one Guatemala's poverty and social injustice represented. By the end of the interview, we were both in tears and hugged one another goodbye.

On the other side of the spectrum, we needed to interview a leader in the intelligence services, one of the agencies responsible for the disappearance of thousands of people during their US-funded civil war. As you can imagine, I had some severe judgments about him. However, I had to choose to kind of 'fall in love' with the guy and the good he was trying to do because if anyone on the planet could spot insincerity, it was that guy. That was his job, so if I wasn't with him from the beginning, I wouldn't get anything useful out of the conversation. Just as it was important to see the whole picture when we were protecting the rivers, the issue in Guatemala was the same. I needed to see the 'whole', which meant I needed to believe that each faction had positive intent (not that there aren't bullies). I chose to believe in him for that particular moment; afterward, I could always not believe in him. It's a method I use to be authentically curious. It means exploring every nook and cranny of their mentality.

This principle of helping things become whole again really involves a lot of healing. It could be healing rifts created through conflict, an imbalance of nature, or healing the psyche. As a trauma, developmental and group psychotherapist, I have experience in the 'healing arts'. I'm not calling myself a healer. People must 'self-heal'; it is just a matter of creating the right conditions, but this work can help them become more whole, individually or collectively. Success here only emerges when we integrate the emotional and intellectual aspects of our humanity.

SOLVING THE UNSOLVABLE

"I don't have bad days, I have challenging days, and that is very different."

Being confronted with adversity, with impossible issues that simply must be solved, comes up repeatedly in my work. My book 'Solving for the Impossible - Harnessing Chaos and Complexity to Heal Business, Society and the Earth' delves into the principle of enabling things to become whole again, across issues, industries, cultures and individuals. It's about recognizing how we, as human beings, have an innate ability to identify and solve complex problems.

When I worked with Hewlett Packard on its global notebook supply chain, they needed to triple their output at a time when parts of it weren't particularly stable. I explained to the chief of staff and the executive team how we would do it, but the supply chain leader said it would be impossible to add that much value in such a short time. I admit I was a little miffed at being doubted, so I said I would do it for free, only pay us if we succeeded. One month later, we got paid.

Solving the unsolvable has also come up in my work as a psychotherapist. Dealing with people who had been tortured, survivors of airplane crashes, and people suffering from combat in war, I was terrified when a psychotic patient was referred to me as their last chance before being institutionalized. It was a seemingly impossible situation, but it never deterred me from helping. She did heal, by the way.

I once had a ballet dancer from The Royal Ballet who, after three surgeries and six different doctors, could no longer perform. After 90 minutes with me, he could perform. I am not saying it's all down to me but the right conditions and identifying what can be done need to be made available in order to heal. Which leads me to…

ROLFING ™ : A LEAPFROG FOR THE BODY

Named after Dr. Ida Rolf, an American biochemist, 'Rolfing' at its most fundamental level, is a series of ten one-hour sessions in which you move methodologically through the different layers of tissue, manipulating the fascia of the body (that tough, stringy stuff you get in a steak) to restore balance. You manipulate the body's fascia to bring the organism back into an alignment and relationship with the field of gravity, which is a fundamental design constraint in the human form.

We are the most upright of all the species, which has all sorts of impacts on people, the physiology, movement, and in some cases, their psychology and self-image. If you take someone whose shoulders are hunched over and whose neck is way ahead of their body, from a physiological point of view, they can't breathe well. When you put the structure back in place, it starts a path to becoming more fully human.

ORGANIZATIONS ARE ORGANISMS

I see organizations as organisms and enable them accordingly by mimicking the "rules" of life itself. In 1987, the computer scientist Craig Reynolds created a computer simulation of starlings' murmuration. These 'Boids', as he called them, followed a few fundamental rules; separation, cohesion, alignment, and avoidance (don't hit something). In doing this, he created a set of rules which allowed complex movement to occur, and, in a way, this can be true of ourselves as individuals and organizations in a complex economic, social, or environmental ecosystem. Some organizations are on the verge of figuring this out.

Looking further into the ecosystem of organizations, I have done a lot of training in 'Holacracy', which focuses on the significant decentralizing of management and distributing authority. It mimics the rules of life itself, allowing organizations to function as an organism in the way that Reynolds mimicked 1000s of starlings flying in perfect harmony. It is currently a new, emerging methodology that doesn't follow the traditional rules of hierarchy, but that is what makes it so efficient.

MY GREATEST TEACHER

I've had many teachers over the years, but I would have to say that my father has probably been the greatest teacher. As a child, you tend to believe in the infallibility of your parents, and then when you get into your teenage years, you begin to realize how human and imperfect they really are. But when my worldview and value system was forming, at around the age of six, my father was a great influence on my intellectual and physical adventures.

Fishing and ranching in South Texas were a bit of a typical boy's dream. At age 6, I was given a pistol and a horse and turned loose to herd cattle. That took a certain amount of confidence on the part of my dad, but that was one of the many situations where I was allowed to take risks and discover things for myself. Once I was allowed to take a small boat into the middle of the Gulf of Mexico and got caught in a storm, a life-threatening situation. Basically, I was just given the freedom to explore. My dad gave me a model of what was possible through athleticism and intellectual prowess, and I think it also leads directly into solving the impossible. Like, 'Go ahead, tell me it's impossible, let's go and see.'

HOW TO BEGIN THE DAY

I begin each day with meditative prayer. I'm a pipe carrier in the Ojibwe, Native American tradition, and that has become the basis of my relationship with Spirit. In the Ojibwe tradition, with each pinch of tobacco is a prayer, and you place it in the bowl of the pipe, smoke it, and the smoke carries prayers between the worlds.

A shaman once said that when you pray, you should weep. It's not just about reciting words, there should be that level of felt sensation, of connection to both the object of your prayer and your intention. That is what I seek in my daily meditative prayer. I go through the parts of my life which I am very grateful for, and it does send me close to tears. Then I choose gratitude and joy every day. When someone at the store says "Have a nice day", my usual answer is "I promise",

I tend to get a smile from that. I don't have bad days, I have challenging days, and that's different. But I don't come home in a foul mood, kick the dog, and yell at my partner.

I play handball competitively and currently rank internationally in the top four for my age group. I have been playing for over 50 years now, and it forces me to run and lift weights, not to drink alcohol, and not to eat sugar. I follow a ketogenic diet, I have been both vegetarian and vegan for several years, but keto now works well for me.

> "We are divine, designed to heal the business side of the Earth."

ONE WITH THE EARTH

In my training as a somatic developmental psychotherapist, I came to understand how we are innately designed to unfold in the seven developmental stages toward the ultimate outcome of mutual connection. The first, existence, is from conception to 3 months after birth. Then there are the developmental stages of getting your needs met, gaining autonomy, and developing 'will', which starts around two years after birth when toddlers begin to establish their boundaries for the first time, and that's a healthy thing to do. Love/sexuality awakens the heart and genital area as energy centers. Opinion forming is the next phase, when you evolve an opinion and express it. The following stages are all about developing a sense of belonging and competitiveness.

I believe we are divinely designed to heal the business side of the Earth, we are built for that. It's a universal unfoldment across cultures, and across time. Of all the qualities embedded in us, the right to exist, to get to know our needs, and get our needs met, to be autonomous, to be able to exercise free will, to be able to be both pragmatic and visionary, to be able to form and express opinions, to be able to be part of a group and still perform at our highest level - our final innate stage is that of mutual connection. That's the work for all of us at this moment in time.

To see more on
Scott Spann

PRIORITIZE EDUCATION AND SKILL DEVELOPMENT

Place emphasis on education and skill development. This focus equips individuals with the necessary knowledge, abilities, and attitude to drive and maximize leapfrogging. Among the core tenets of leapfrogging, one stands out for its transformative potential: Prioritizing Education and Skill Development. As we plot the trajectory of our progress, it is vital to understand that education and skills are the fuel that drives the engine of innovation and change.

> *"Education is the passport to the future, for tomorrow belongs to those who prepare for it today."*
>
> *Malcolm X*

NATIONAL COUNTRY PROGRAMS

Singapore's SkillsFuture initiative is a national movement that seeks to enable all Singaporeans to develop to their fullest potential throughout life, and realize their aspirations by taking advantage of a wide range of opportunities in the continually evolving economy.

CORPORATES

IBM's P-TECH school model stands out as an innovative approach in corporate education initiatives. Through this program, IBM provides mentorship and skill development opportunities to students, aligning their curriculum with real-world job requirements.

NEW VENTURES AND STARTUPS

Coursera, an online education platform, has made world-class education accessible to millions across the globe. The startup offers courses from top universities, helping people acquire new skills and enhance their career prospects.

LOCAL COMMUNITY CHANGE

In rural Kenya, the M-PESA Foundation Academy offers a unique learning environment that fosters leadership and entrepreneurship among its students, enabling local communities to drive sustainable change.

INDIVIDUAL PERSONAL

Malala Yousafzai, a Pakistani activist for female education and the youngest-ever Nobel Prize laureate, used education as her leapfrogging tool to transform the world's perception of girls' education.

To equip our societies for the leapfrogging journey, we must ensure that education and skill development are not just priorities but imperatives. As we incorporate this value into our collective consciousness, we'll forge a path that enables everyone to contribute meaningfully to the innovative future.

ROCCO SHIELDS

CEO, Genius Academy

Rocco Shields is an internationally acclaimed, award-winning filmmaker and short-form content creator who believes passionately in the power of storytelling to change the world for the better.

From the age of three, she has been in love with being behind the camera and orchestrating those stories. With an auspicious career mapped out for her as a director and producer in the entertainment industry, Rocco decided to change her trajectory. In 2008, she began creating educational media for the first online program from a major accredited university. Utilizing digital technology and cameras, which at the time were revolutionizing the film industry, Rocco created engaging and visual educational content that looked nothing like the stuffy "high school history class" content seen in schools previously.

Rocco's short film 'Love is All You Need?' (2013) went viral on the internet, depicting an alternate society where heterosexuality was considered sinful, and homosexuality was the cultural norm. The film's narrative provided wisdom and insight into bullying and prejudice in the modern era and could be regarded as Rocco's leapfrog moment, as she was able to evaluate how audiences reacted to the piece. Rocco then made it her mission to make equally well-crafted cinematic experiences available to educators and institutions to challenge and transform how people think, learn, and feel about the issues that affect audiences today.

As CEO of Genius Academy, a hybrid content creation and instructional design studio with an on-demand streaming platform, she is making content that lies at the heart of some of the most prestigious online programmes in the world, transforming education into experiential learning that engages and educates students.

She states "I'm proud to say that some people even call it 'binge-worthy education'!"

Rocco in her own words...

STORY STORY STORY

The biggest thing I learned from the film industry is 'story, story, story'. Audiences are always drawn to a story - when you ask a friend to watch a film with you, they usually ask "what's it about?" not whether it was filmed in 4k with lots of special effects. I'm focused on how people relate to a story, and how I can make people feel like they're in it.

As a filmmaker, if I can get an audience invested in a fictional or fantasy world, I can certainly get them to care about the realities of their own world. We do that with music, lighting, sound effects, and a whole lot of cinematic language tools designed to get people engaged and keep them engaged until the very end. Whether we realize it or not, audiences are expected to pick up on social cues, observe the characters' modeled behavior, and apply that to following the narrative. We don't switch our brains off when we are watching a film or television programme, it is hardly a passive activity. If it was, it wouldn't matter what we watched.

> "As a filmmaker, if I can get an audience invested in a fictional or fantasy world I can certainly get them to care about the realities of their own world."

Anybody could be a screenwriter or filmmaker if they learn the tools of engagement, but for a story to work, the audience has to be led down a path, exposed to new ideas and concepts and taught the rules of the world in which the story takes place. These lessons are applied during the film's two-hour runtime and aren't easily forgotten after the lights turn on.

With educational media, the concept is the same. We work with educators and instructional designers to ensure the lessons explored align with the learning objectives for the course or program we are serving.

LEAPFROGGING

What I learned from the film industry and how it can directly relate to education is summed up by Thomas Edison when he said "life is all what you focus on. Learn lessons and keep moving forwards towards your goals and dreams."

There's a whole world of cinematic language that Hollywood has been refining for the last one hundred years, and it's all about making us connect to the story and characters, making us feel like we're in their shoes, feeling everything those characters are feeling. We learn from that. So I thought, if we can do that for entertainment, why can't we also do it for education?

Edison said: "remember, life is all what you focus on. Learn lessons and keep moving forwards towards your goals and dreams."

I put my theory to the test in my film 'Love is All You Need?' I was deeply troubled to see how many young people were committing suicide just because they loved differently to what society expected from them. I turned the social norms around to where it was normal to be gay and taboo to be straight. I had so many straight people tell me after they saw the film that their opinions on gay people had changed. I knew I had my answer, and that lesson about the power of cinematic language leapfrogged me into bringing that knowledge to some of the best universities across the nation, and now to Genius Academy.

Jesus taught with parables for a reason. It's just that today our modern-day parables are seen and heard on video.

A SHIFT IN THINKING

It has become abundantly clear to me that immersive, experiential learning is the key to driving student success, and that's why we look at the curriculum not just as a series of lessons but as a storyline that can carry a learner from their first day of class all the way to the completion of the program.

The media and interactive content we build supplements the core learning principles, and presents the content to students in a way they can easily digest, connect with, and commit to memory. Our approach has been proven to lead to higher competency scores, increased learning retention, and better student outcomes.

The biggest success comes from our content that best reflects the realities of the work in the field the learners are preparing for. As experiential learning tools, this media acts as a simulation of sorts. Students utilizing this type of media are engaged throughout the learning process and find themselves better prepared for success in the classroom and ultimately, in the workplace.

Why is experiential learning so effective? Research shows that 63% of people remembered facts better when they were presented within the context of a story. Yet, only 5% remembered the information when it was presented in a traditional learning format. That's a massive difference.

It's all about the brain and our neural pathways. Let's say we were just watching a PowerPoint presentation with boring bullet points. Two parts of the brain get activated: the Broca's area and Wernicke's area, which are both aligned to speech. Basically, it hits our language processing areas where we decode words into meaning, and that's it - nothing else happens.

But, when we are told a story, not only does it engage the language-processing areas of our brain, it also engages other areas too, creating something called cognitive empathy - the same emotions that are engaged when we watch TV shows or films. This relates specifically to perspective and memory performance. Compelling storytelling also causes our brains to fire up and release cortisol, which helps with awareness. The cortisol triggers dopamine, which induces pleasure, and then oxytocin, which in combination with cortisol, dopamine, and other chemicals in our storytelling cocktail, helps us start to feel emotion.

A simplified relatable experience is when you hear a certain song on the radio and it takes you back to the place where you heard it the first time. How many of us have had this experience? The same happens when we watch TV, film, or other immersive media experiences that engage our senses.

AN IDEA TO CHANGE THE WORLD

I have always believed that no matter where a person comes from, everyone deserves the best education. The challenge I posed for Genius Academy was to change the world. The way it has done this is by democratizing education. I've set up a model that makes our content affordable to anyone who wants the very best in educational materials. Traditional education, with its reliance on textbooks and lectures, has served us well for generations, but educators and learners are not reaching their full potential when it comes to discovering and exploring new concepts.

We have managed to overcome these limitations by using technology and narrative techniques borrowed from the film industry. With the introduction of the Genius Academy platform, we have made this groundbreaking content available to all institutions and learners everywhere.

No longer is high-quality, dynamic educational media strictly limited to organizations with significant endowments and resources. Digital content creation, online learning, and streaming media all contribute to this democratization of education, where the doors are open for everybody, and access is granted to all who want to pursue it

"Digital content creation, online learning and streaming media all contribute to this democratization of education."

ROCCO'S TAKEAWAY

It is often said that education is the key to changing the world, and I believe that wholeheartedly.

Traditionally, the problem has been in overcoming the obstacles and preconceived notions that are ingrained in so many of us. Visionaries and educators have the power to bring people together in pursuit of creating a better future. People with vision have the ability to see what other people cannot.

This is much like the thought leaders who have transformed the world. We share one commonality, we are all human with ideas larger than ourselves, but finding a way to connect and get the message out to the masses has always been a challenge. How do we communicate and educate in a way that resonates with everyone?

Any great idea or concept has to get out of your head and be shared with the world. Because if nobody knows about it, how is anything going to change? That's the catch. It's hard to change the world by yourself, so not only do you need to get that idea out of your head, you also have to be able to communicate it effectively so it can inspire others. I believe the most effective way to do this is through storytelling, and that can easily be done by using the tried and tested technology of cinema and the art of cinematic engagement. I truly believe that this is the most noble and important use of media and storytelling, as it has the power to bring us together and to model the right way to move forward and make changes that benefit us all.

We can and will come together as a collective if the message is clear. Together, there is no limit to what we can accomplish.

"Education is the key to changing the world."

To see more on
Rocco Shields

KIAN SEAH

CEO at HHI | Fulbright Scholar | Certified Ocean Bound Plastics Recycler
YPO Malaysia | Endeavor Entrepreneur

There is an old saying, "Where there's muck, there's money," a point Kian Seah knows well. At ten years old, when most of his friends were in a field playing basketball, he was in his parent's backyard earning money by separating recyclables that his parents had collected from households. At a very young age, he learned how to create value from people's rubbish and has been doing that ever since.

At that time, recycling was not a word associated with conservation, civic duty, or environmentalism. It was perhaps considered a lowly career prospect, so much so that Kian's parents were too embarrassed to have the word in their job titles, and did everything they could to dissuade their children not to follow in their footsteps. Their efforts were unsuccessful as all their children went into what is now regarded as a worthwhile, profitable endeavor to ensure our world is kept clean, beautiful, and thriving. It's truly a family affair, with Kian's brother recycling paper, another brother in scrap metal, and a sister dealing with aluminum, stainless steel, and copper. Plastic, however, has remained the domain of Kian at Heng Hiap Industries (HHI).

Today, 'Reduce, Reuse, Recycle' is a very different matter. One could argue that recycling is now one of the most important jobs of the 21st century, especially considering that humans have amassed 7 billion tons of plastic waste. Plastic is now so pervasive in the global environment that scientific research is identifying microplastics in the human body.

The concept of rubbish collection has seen a dramatic shift from when Kian was a young boy. Long gone is the negative stereotype of the work-worn, solitary man in grubby clothes throwing rubbish into his truck and manually sifting through the debris, hoping to find something of value. It's now a multi-million-pound business, a science-based, high-tech, logistical operation led by well-educated and forward-thinking individuals doing their part to save our planet. Kian's company leads the way in this progressive approach. Today HHI has collected up to 60,000 tons of plastic and intends to collect 100,000 tons within the next two years. Digitization is critical to its efficiency, HHI developed an app allowing households to order waste collections, a far cry from the pen, paper, and verbal negotiations of yesteryear. It's no accident that Kian's associate metal and paper recycling companies are one of the two largest scrap metal suppliers to local steel mills, including Singapore, and one of the two largest scrap paper suppliers to local paper mills.

However, his innovation and creative thinking are probably the most impressive elements of Kian's story. His company has developed 17 breakthrough technologies, one of which is transforming scrap plastic into 'smart plastic' which can be used in niche operations. Ocean-bound plastic is now also being used in everyday products from major global brands, and he intends to also transform plastics into renewable energy, which would be a game changer. His company is the first in the world to be awarded the Ocean Bound Plastic (OBP) certification by Zero Plastic Oceans.

"Plastic is now so pervasive in the global environment that scientific research is identifying microplastics in the human body."

Kian in his own words...

FROM SCRAP TO SMART

We are based in Malaysia and convert scrap plastics into 'smart' plastics, which include high melt, fire retardant, and anti-bacterial variants. We are currently working with top electronics makers from Korea, top home appliance makers from Japan, and top industrial handling makers from the EU, resulting in up to 70% of our end products being exported to 38 countries.

The procedure of recycling plastic is broken down into six independent processes; collection, separation, crushing, mixing, washing, and finally, extrusion. If we think of it as a value chain, there is a high dependency on labor and a lot of idling capacity, as well as an absence of an established standard to govern how the independent processes could work efficiently together. Creating a vertical integration system has helped to reduce labor costs and idling time. Most importantly, we have created an internal standard which has been shared with our independent recycling operators and has now become the industrial playbook.

"The key thing is about co-creating the value and creating an ecosystem from there, where we are not necessarily just focusing on the product, but looking at the process as a whole."

Marine pollution has specific complexities, and we confront that by extending the vertical with a horizontal integration system through mechanical recycling. We convert what cannot be mechanically recycled into biodiesel, or circular naphtha (the raw material that creates plastic), through chemical recycling. This process allows us to be the largest ocean-bound plastic collector and recycler.

Chemical recycling has traditionally had a bad reputation, mainly because of the process of exposing the materials to extreme temperatures, which can be harmful to the environment due to emissions. However, HHI has been able to bypass the refinery stage to create an environmentally clean chemical recycling process that cuts costs and produces completely fossil-free materials derived from recovered ocean plastic.

Although not the highest on the list, Malaysia is one of the top ten ocean-polluting countries. And one of the reasons HHI has been inspired to come up with a solution to the issue is to ensure Malaysia is removed from this discouraging line-up. Leakage is the main culprit; unmanaged or poorly managed waste finds its way to the ocean. We work with scuba divers and organizations such as River Clean-up to intercept and capture the plastic material within 50km of the shoreline.

THE EXTRAORDINARY RESULT OF COLLABORATION TO LEAPFROG

Recycling technologies have been evolving very quickly, and removing and upcycling materials is getting much better regarding quality. Now we are seeing materials like polypropylene and polyethylene achieving food-grade status. The technology will continue to develop, and the process of recycling will also continue to improve. For instance, we are currently working with Capgemini, an expert in digital transformation, to pilot a system where we can work in unison with the mobile pickers, the yard owner, the processor, and the aggregator. We are hoping that by using a digital platform, the entire material flow, whether it's metal, paper, or plastic, can be properly mapped, so the process will become transparent, unified, and dynamic and, most importantly, we will be able to redistribute the value according to contribution across the chain.

Working with Capgemini is just one example of how we can collaborate with partners to improve the recycling process. Another example is SABIC which had already aspired to use alternative circular feedstock to make a circular polymer, where the source comes from recycled materials. I discussed with them my desire to create a material so clean that the circular naphtha could bypass the refinery stage, and we started our collaboration and launched the product. Sabic used this circular feedstock or naphtha derived from ocean-bound plastic from ocean-feeding waterways for the first time in their European operations. They've commercialized it and launched it as Ocean Bound. Collaboration can create extraordinary results.

A PLASTIC NEUTRAL WORLD

We are a global supplier, exporting to 38 countries to companies like LG and Panasonic. As Malaysia is still a developing country, we do not get a lot of incentives or help from the government. We get some innovation grants and some green financing, but that's about it. The key thing is about co-creating the value and creating an ecosystem from there, where we are not necessarily just focusing on the product but looking at the process as a whole. We need to focus on it as a circulatory system. As a team, we are constantly thinking about the future and how humankind and plastic will co-exist. There can only really be two outcomes. One is to become a plastic-free world, and the other is to become a plastic-neutral world. It's a bit like being carbon neutral by ensuring that the plastic we use is collected and recycled, therefore, decreasing the environmental impact. And plastic is an amazing, magical material. It can be collected, separated, crushed, mixed, and converted into the raw material. And every time the form and shape are changed, it gives value. Even when the molecular structure has diminished, it still provides value through chemical recycling and can give value indefinitely. The issue is not with plastic because if plastic is recycled, it adds value to our lives. The problem is with our ability to continue with the scenario where we are reducing, recycling, and reusing in a circular fashion, instead of allowing used plastic to seep into an ocean where it could stay for hundreds of years. That is the essence of the problem regarding plastic.

We need to reduce our dependence on fossil fuels, and to do this, we will have to collectively act like jugglers, ensuring that the plastic we use gets converted. If we move away from a linear perspective and start to concentrate on a circular life cycle, plastic has the potential to become a resource with one of the lower carbon footprints. It seems an extraordinary claim but an undeniable fact.

> "We need to reduce our dependence on fossil fuels, and in order to do this we have to collectively act like a juggler, ensuring that the plastic we use gets converted."

MY LEAPFROG IDEA FOR THE WORLD

All we have to do is recognize how important this circulatory process of recycling and reusing is to live in harmony with this magical medium we call plastic.

I deny that we have a plastic pollution problem. What I think we have is a plastic ignorance problem. Plastic is not the culprit here, it's human interaction.

To see more on
Kian Seah

INSIST ON ETHICAL AND RESPONSIBLE INNOVATION

Maintain ethical considerations at the forefront of leapfrogging initiatives. This approach ensures the responsible use of technology, data privacy, and safeguards against unintended consequences. In the endeavor to leapfrog, we must always be reminded of an essential principle: Insist on Ethical and Responsible Innovation. The accelerated pace of development should not come at the cost of our moral obligations. The sanctity of ethical considerations remains our guiding light, keeping us on the path of responsible progress.

"The real problem of humanity is the following: we have Paleolithic emotions, medieval institutions, and god-like technology."

E. O. Wilson

NATIONAL COUNTRY PROGRAMS

The EU's General Data Protection Regulation (GDPR) sets a benchmark for data privacy and ethics globally. It is a clear mandate that innovation cannot be prioritized over privacy rights.

CORPORATES

Microsoft's Responsible AI initiative exemplifies a corporate commitment to ethics in technology. The company has implemented AI ethics guidelines and rigorous responsible AI practices across its operations to ensure technology is developed and deployed responsibly.

NEW VENTURES AND STARTUPS

OpenAI, a research organization dedicated to creating and promoting friendly AI, is committed to long-term safety and technical leadership to ensure artificial general intelligence (AGI) benefits all of humanity.

LOCAL COMMUNITY CHANGE

In South Africa, Project Isizwe advocates for affordable internet access, demonstrating a commitment to digital inclusion, data privacy, and responsible connectivity.

INDIVIDUAL PERSONAL

As an individual example, Timnit Gebru, a leading AI ethicist, has been a vocal advocate for ethics in AI, pushing for more scrutiny into biases in AI systems.

As we continue our journey towards leapfrogging, maintaining an unwavering commitment to ethical and responsible innovation is paramount. In doing so, we ensure that our leaps forward are safe, fair, and beneficial to all.

ESTHER O'CALLAGHAN OBE

Founder - hundo.xyz
GTA Metaverse Lead - GTA Metaverse

With a strong social conscience and a wide array of interests and talents, Esther O'Callaghan OBE has a list of achievements too long to mention. As the first female DJ/Producer to own an independent vinyl store, she is also a qualified Level 2 British Triathlon Federation coach, a speaker at international events, and an angel investor. She has over 20 years of experience in the government, arts, culture, and music sectors, throughout which she has worked on youth issues such as homelessness, teenage self-harm, young male suicide prevention, and unemployment.

As a child growing up in a single-parent family on free school meals in Blackpool, Esther experienced first-hand the poverty trap and, although bright enough to pursue academia, left school at 16 to start working. From bar work, care homes, and learning support for young people with special educational needs, all the way to fundraising and grant-making, her passion for music, especially vinyl, remained consistent.

Esther was the first female DJ/producer to own an independent, specialist record shop with a focus on making women welcome in a typically male-dominated arena. Later, Esther founded the Factory Foundation, a charity that initially provided DJ and mixing courses for 14-16 year olds in deprived areas. It wasn't just a fluffy youth club providing decks to muck about on, it was a formal 8-week course that taught disaffected young people about the music industry, providing them with an accreditation to add to their CVs, and a performance to showcase their talent. This well focused endeavor won her the Clarins 'Most Dynamic Woman of the Year' Award in 2005.

She is also the recipient of numerous other awards, including being one of the youngest civilians at 26 years old to receive an OBE (2007/8) for her voluntary work, being made a Freeman of the City of London, and being named Liveryman of the Worshipful Company of Tin Plate, alias Wireworkers (2019). She was also included in the SIA Global Power List 150 (2018) and the Barclays Women of the Year Alumni (2018).

Youth and employment have been the foundation of most of her philanthropic endeavors. Esther is a successful entrepreneur who could easily have followed the money, but instead chose to follow an alternative path that was about doing good, giving back, and improving the lives of thousands of young people. She is one of these rare people who will undoubtedly leave a positive and lasting mark on the world.

"The best use of technology is when it aligns with your personal goals or growth."

Esther in her own words...

THE FUTURE OF TECH

The best use of technology is when it aligns with your personal goals or growth. If you need web3, crypto, NFT or a metaverse strategy to help you move forward, then it works well. However, just jumping on the bandwagon, and rushing out a collection just because everyone else is, is futile. You need a business strategy that underpins the need.

At hundo, we validate and verify qualifications using non-fungible tokens (NFTs) in a digital skills wallet. It's a technology which is very much aligned with what we do as an EdTech company. So using NFTs means micro-credentials and qualifications can be minted onto blockchain, creating a permanent validated and verified record of skills and competencies.

hundo aims to educate young people in a virtual space and partner them with educators, brands and employers. Each time an individual completes a course on any platform, they can add it to their hundo digital skills wallet as an NFT. We are using the technology to remove the need for a CV/resume and to give young people and employers a more efficient, effective way to match skills both now and in the future.

Along with the NFT-based skills wallet, all hundo learners create their avatar based profile. Again, this is about bringing new technology (and its future application) to the broadest possible audience. We fundamentally believe that an increasingly immersive online experience will become the norm and having a digital identity that is cross-platform and interoperable will be a key part of that.

"According to the World Economic Forum, there are 1.1 billion new tech roles needed by 2030."

THE FUTURE OF ED-TECH

I founded hundo.xyz to enable young people, parents, educators and employers to discover the future of learning and work. Its remit is to enhance compulsory education with the employability experience and skills needed across frontier tech.

According to the World Economic Forum, there will be 1.1 billion new tech roles needed by 2030, with employers saying they are desperate for talent now. At the same time, we have the first ever digital native generation, which is facing rising levels of unemployment. In response to this incongruity, hundo is developing a blended learning platform that augments current education with access to the skills needed for work, promoting them to employers and brands that are actively hiring. We do this at our annual on-demand content stream, CareerCon, the world's first immersive career expo for Gen Z.

The way we all work, live, learn, and earn is being disrupted, and we built hundo to be the bridge for young people, educators, and employers to cross that divide. This is also why we deliberately built it as a web2 > web3 platform. To access hundo and attend CareerCon, you don't need an expensive laptop or a headset. Web3 is still emerging, it's not like one day we'll all wake up and suddenly the internet is now the metaverse. But preparing people ahead of time for what a more immersive world looks like and how they can be part of it, is what we set out to achieve.

LEAPFROGGING

Everything I have done since starting my career has led me to eventually leapfrog into what I am doing now. From having the record shop in Manchester to setting up a youth music project to support young people to stay in education. Running the first simultaneous live broadcast for Radio 1 and OneXtra and going on to produce Gorillaz: Demon Days Live as part of the Manchester International Festival. Then I produced 'Thirty One Songs' to raise money for CALM (Campaign Against Living Miserably), the UK's suicide helpline.

I would love to say it was all planned, but for me, I see things in the world that could be better and try to use my skills to be part of making that happen, with varying degrees of success and failure.

So being involved with these youth based projects has really leapfrogged me into what I do now, which is still all about supporting young people. I'm a big advocate for transferable skills, especially now that careers are increasingly non-linear. Having had such a varied career myself, I have found that it's been very beneficial to become a start-up founder because I spend more than half my time doing things I've never done before.

It is ironic that I stopped touring and DJ-ing because of the amount of time I spent on the road, and now, as a start-up founder, I am on the road even more than I was back then. I also do a lot of public speaking, and have found that being on stage is definitely easier because of my prior experience, but on the whole, I much prefer, and find it easier to play records than public speaking.

INSPIRATION

"When it comes to finding inspiration, for me, listening to and learning from children and young people is a good start, as they usually seem to have the best ideas and solutions."

When it comes to finding inspiration, for me, listening to and learning from children and young people is a good start, as they usually seem to have the best ideas and solutions. That's one of the reasons why I started hundo - to help equip them with the skills, knowledge, and opportunities they need.

I am also inspired by people who reinvent themselves and refuse to be labeled. One of these people in particular, is Bruce Lee. Mainly because of his level of work, discipline, and determination against all the odds - developing grit and resilience to withstand what life throws at all of us.

For me, Dr Seuss's 'Oh The Places You'll Go' is one of the all time best self-help books ever written, and there is a fair amount of leapfrogging in there too. When things get really tough, that is my go to book for inspiration, which usually gets me back on track.

To see more on
Esther O'Callaghan OBE

Esther O'Callaghan OBE

IPSHITA KUMAR

Co-founder – Lemonade

If Ipshita Kumar were to go to a networking event for Indian women in tech, she'd be one of a small group. That group would be even smaller if the event was for Web3. She is quick to proclaim that South Asian women and tech are still very much an anomaly, so much so that Ipshita has had to create her own narrative and become a role model to others entering the sphere. Her seemingly unorthodox pathway is not so surprising when you look at the success of her mother who reinvented herself at the age of 50 with her own highly successful online Ayurveda business.

As a student, Ipshita studied dance, arts and culture before moving into hospitality and tourism where she later worked across the world in 5 star hotels. She admits this experience has coloured her creative flair, and has left her highly influenced by arts and cultural knowledge.

Following in her mum's entrepreneurial spirit and ability to push personal boundaries, Ipshita is a co-founder of a Web3 based events platform called Lemonade. A concept which brings people together, builds communities and monetises collaborative efforts. Her story began in her lounge in Barcelona where she set up an offline event. This quickly escalated to 20 Lemonade stands in New York, Delhi and London. The pandemic could have been the death knell for any business reliant on close contact gatherings, but Ipshita and her co-founders were able to pivot the model quickly by going virtual.

Ipshita in her own words...

THE FUTURE IS FEMALE

I currently work at Hype as VP for Brand Innovation. It's the largest remote crypto marketing agency and the entire leadership team is made up of 60% women. Also, Lemonade is over 50% women, so things have turned around quickly. There was a time not so long ago when roles such as Head of Developer Relations, Head of Product, or Head of Marketing would have been associated with men, but now they are becoming a female-led domain. So we're developing a lot of workshops to offer free daily knowledge to as many women as possible. I also work with Allbright, a collective run by and for women. It started off as a private membership club based in London but has now transitioned into a digital arena. So I'm working with them to build modules and curate Web3 learning experiences so more women can make waves in the metaverse irrespective of what their current knowledge or experience has been in the space.

WEB3 AND NFTS

Marketing and the way we do business has been transformed. If we just look at marketing and the way we interact, the way we position brands, it's all changed. NFTs (Non-Fungible Tokens) are just a simple line of code that is stored on a digital ledger that verifies the proof of ownership and creation for

> "We're developing a lot of workshops to offer our free daily knowledge to as many women as possible."

> "Profit for us is secondary, it's more about doing things properly and being in the forefront of change."

any asset on the blockchain. And the user facing element of it can be music, art or even just a membership card, in fact it can be anything you want. As we move forward, everything will be stored on the blockchain, so instead of listening to music on Spotify for example, you will listen to it on the blockchain.

There is a real cultural element to NFTs, because everything will be stored as an NFT, all assets will essentially become NFTs. For instance, the transaction of purchasing an object like a ceramic cup can be recorded. It then has an NFT, a digital twin, an asset of its own. The demand and supply is dictated the same way as basic economics. So for example, if you're buying a house, it's an asset, something personal to you, it holds a lot more value in a personal sense. When people buy monkey JPEGs, or NFT doodles, it's because they have a specific personal value. That value dictates the demand and supply and also the price point. If you look at NFTs as a baseline technology, this specific technology enables you to record assets on the blockchain, own things in real life, but also have a digital ownership footprint of it.

ADVISORY BOARDS

Coming from South Asia, I grew up in a very disciplined environment. From the age of 5, I would get up at 6am every morning, spend about half an hour reading a book, then I would have breakfast. That level of discipline has stayed with me in adulthood, and has really helped whilst working remotely.

Yoga and meditation is also something that I grew up with. It's becoming more popular today in the western world, but it's something I have done since I was very young and continue to do today. Following a disciplined schedule like getting up early, yoga and eating well are all things I learned from my Indian culture. I also identify people who I admire and respect and ask them to be on my advisory board. The board changes every 2 years depending on my career path, and it really helps with self-affirmation and having a sense of belonging. Just knowing that there are other people, in particular other women around the globe, who are happy to support me makes me feel less alone.

EMOTIONAL QUOTIENT

I originally come from New Delhi but have lived in 6 different countries and I have lived through the difference in behaviour between people from different cultures. For example, the way people behave socially and professionally in Dubai is very different to the way people behave in Spain or India. This difference is magnified now that we work remotely. Understanding and decoding what people write for instance can be challenging and it means developing a new set of soft skills. In particular the skill of being able to understand, comprehend and deliver back on someone's emotions. For instance, when I was working in the hospitality industry and guests were angry if their order wasn't quite right, or they weren't happy with their room, I would need to stay calm and continue to be empathetic towards them. Being able to respond back by showing the right level of compassion so they feel heard whilst also being able to put my own point across is a skill in itself. It's all about having a certain level of emotional quotient, which, by the way, a lot of intelligent people lack.

SHARING FAILURE

I am relatively early on in my career but am still able to distribute my knowledge and experience to a wider audience through LinkedIn, Facebook, TikTok and Instagram. These social media platforms have worked well in distributing as much knowledge and education as possible. It's great to be able to share thought leadership with people I wouldn't naturally have come into contact with. But, for me, the most important aspect is being able to share stories of failure. When you're open to sharing the learnings you have obtained from failing, you become more approachable and people are more likely to reach out to you, so it becomes a magnet.

Everyday I am trying a path I have never experienced before so I am bound to make mistakes. The important thing is being able to learn from those mistakes. I've been lucky in having the right mentors and colleagues who are open minded when it comes to making mistakes, so having that mindset in my surroundings is very important.

THE SECRET OF MY SUCCESS

There have been a number of people who have been integral to my success. Firstly, Casey, one of my flatmates when I was based in Barcelona. He had an in-depth understanding and experience in product building and became the co-founder of Lemonade. At the time I was still in hospitality and had not yet transitioned into tech, so he held my hand for a good couple of years and was really pivotal to Lemonade's success. Cressida has been part of my personal advisory board for the longest time. She's the Chief Commercial Officer at Travel Tech and has been guiding and supporting me in my leadership style, how to scale things up and just general advice. I know it's a cliche, but nevertheless true, my mom has been a great inspiration to me. Her background is in fashion, in particular leather manufacturing, but then at

"Everyday I am trying a path I have never experienced before so I am bound to make mistakes. The important thing is being able to learn from those mistakes so they don't get repeated."

the age of 50 years she discovered LinkedIn and started her own virtual business based in Switzerland. She's a power-woman and very special.

To see more on
Ipshita Kumar

CHANDRAN NAIR

Founder of Global Institute for Tomorrow,
Consultant, Author, Entrepreneur, Sports coach

A Consultant, author, public speaker, and entrepreneur, as well as the founder of Asia's leading independent think tank (Global Institute for Tomorrow), Chandran is an outspoken advocate for alternative and more plural world views. He has authored a number of compelling books, including *Consumptionomics* which The Guardian considers to be one of the top-fifty break out capitalism books, *The Sustainable State*, which examines the future of government, economy and society, and his latest book, *Dismantling Global White Privilege*, which has been recommended by the FT as one of the best reads of 2022.

As an individual who seeks to create a more equitable world, he has also created 'The Other Hundred', a non-profit book project which serves as an alternative to the Forbes 100 and other media rich lists.

Chandran in his own words...

INTELLECTUAL DISHONESTY

I come from a different place in terms of consciousness, and found myself unwilling to be associated with mainstream ideas. All too often these narratives perpetuate western ideological beliefs and even lies dressed up as PR to deceive the masses. For example, I don't believe there is a net-zero carbon future (it is unscientific), I don't believe our rights and freedoms can be unfettered, and I also don't believe in the democratization of everything. After all, even businesses are not democracies, they are more authoritarian and less likely to embrace diversity and inclusion despite the posturing. It's all just part of a big lie, one that most of us are all too ready to buy into in order to avoid confronting inconvenient truths in our daily lives.

My world view has primarily been shaped by my childhood in Malaysia, and its multicultural environment, despite being a product of British colonialism. As a Hindu child, I would get up at 6.30 am, and pray to the gods (some of which were depicted in mythology as an elephant, lion or monkey) in Sanskrit, a language I didn't understand. Then I would be off to the missionary school, where I would recite the lord's prayer and be taught by white men that God was, in fact, white with blonde hair and blue eyes.

"The future is biological, not digital. Toilets before more mobile connectivity."

This dual experience made me versatile, flexible and open-minded in accepting the dichotomy of my daily existence. My home was a small village with a mosque nearby, and when I walked through it, the Imam would give me sweets. The daily Muslim call for prayer (Adhan) felt reassuring as a child, so now, when I see a Muslim with a beard, a skull cap and a long gown or hijab, I don't cross the street because I don't see them as a threat, I see them as my brothers and sisters. The same goes for my Chinese friends, who I have a lot of respect for. I do not share the western world's paranoia about China. In my eyes, I see the Chinese as respectful, hard working people with an ancient civilization. My diverse experiences as a child gave me this independence of thought, so I don't need the Americans or Europeans telling me who is a threat to my freedom.

FREEDOM FIGHTER

My first experience of flying was at the age of twenty when I went to the UK. It was a revelation for me to see white men digging roads, and my mindset was leapfrogged into a different realm of awareness about the world we live in. I also became aware of how little the average Brit knew about the rest of the world, and became bored with the casual racism in Britain at that time. I was developing quickly from a political standpoint and became involved in the anti-apartheid movement of the early eighties. As a biochemical engineer, I was able to move to Southern Africa, as I was interested in development work (water and sanitation), but I was also keen to learn more about the liberation struggles, and wanted to do my bit to support it.

During the day, I would build rural water supply and sanitation systems, and by night I would contribute to the underground movement. Some may have called me a terrorist, others, a supporter of the liberation struggle.

After almost a decade, including 4 years in Thailand, I moved to Hong Kong, where I found myself working for one of the world's leading environmental consulting firms called ERM, where I became the regional chairman, expanding the company into 22 offices in 12 countries, with a total of about 600 employees. Another leapfrog moment was the realization that my perspectives about globalization and equity differed greatly from most of my western board members, many of whom for instance even supported the Iraq war. So, in 2004, I resigned and started the Global Institute for Tomorrow.

DISMANTLING GLOBAL WHITE PRIVILEGE

A number of historical events influenced my journey towards understanding the issues of economic power, hegemony and equity. The imprisonment of Nelson Mandela, the anti-apartheid movement and the wars in Mozambique, Rhodesia, all shined a light on how white privilege distorts societies around the world. White privilege is embedded in the very nature of major global institutions, and what is called globalization in the rules-based order. Its result is that the dominance of western institutions and western culture have now become so pervasive throughout the world, that even many non-white people have internalized it, viewing themselves through the lens of what is deemed acceptable by the West. When we look at the media, for the most part, white cultural products remain the aspirational standard. In this sense, I believe white privilege needs to be dismantled to create a post-western world that has less conflict and most importantly more equitable.

Today, we've reached a stage of 'dumbing down' in the consumer-driven global economy, to the point where we care more about what celebrities and royalty think and wear than we do about global inequality or the environment. It is critically important that we reject the consumption-driven neoliberal economic model of the western

> "You can't leapfrog unless you are also willing to go to dark corners and live with demons."

world. By 2050, Asia will be the most populated part of the world, so I believe it is imperative that we reject this American dream of consumerism under the guise of innovation and progress. If Asia and Africa adopt the American model of consumption-driven growth, we can say goodbye to the fight against climate change and other existential threats we face. You do not need to be a rocket scientist to understand this.

THE COLLECTIVE VERSUS THE INDIVIDUAL

When we live in a world where up to four billion people do not have access to basic necessities, we need to appreciate the importance of redefining our rights. The future should be more biological, rather than technological. As an engineer, I'm not anti-technology, but if Asia copies the western economic model, the future of the planet will be very bleak. The purpose of technology should be to protect the biosphere, not destroy it for corporate greed.

The voodoo economics of 'buy one, get one free' created by technology encourages people to buy things they don't need with money they don't have. So, my political philosophy is to reject the western fixation with democracy, free markets, unfettered GDP growth, and the concept of the individual as king. As a counterexample to this model, Japan is a democratic society, but people understand the collective versus the individual. The rights of the individual need to be subservient to the collective interests of society. That is the foundation from which you are able to leapfrog.

BASIC RIGHTS

When we consider the basic rights of life, it's not about more digital technology or cars, or other consumer products, it is essentially about food, safety, security, basic energy needs, water and sanitation. Especially as we are in the post-pandemic era, I believe that basic hygiene will become the most important right, which means water supply and sanitation. Imagine that up to 80% of the world's wastewater today is left untreated to acceptable standards.

As an engineer, I would argue that initially we should be building water supply systems and wastewater treatment plants on a global scale, and having done that, putting fiber optics in the sewers to ensure true global connectivity. I would argue that Draconian measures will be needed to allow everyone to have basic rights like housing, and enough electricity to lead dignified lives, healthcare and education to escape the drudgery of life. That's how a country like China achieved this for 95% of its population. They have a very different political system to the western world, and it works for them.

INSPIRATIONS

Many people have inspired me at different points in my life. One was Muhammad Ali, who came to Malaysia when he was at the peak of his career, spoke about the Vietnam War, which was raging in my part of the world, in Southeast Asia. Other inspirations have been the Vietnamese leader Ho Chi Minh and Fidel Castro who both fought against oppression. I learned that having a non-western view is not the same as having an anti-western perspective, and it is important not to be bullied with such accusations.

READING AND WRITING

"The most important thing for me is to start the day the night before, by believing tomorrow will be a good day."

Although I have written a few books and have, in the past, been an avid reader, I found myself reading less these past couple of years, mainly because there's nothing new being said in mainstream, western media and books. In fact the obvious distortions, and the lack of intellectual honesty or even ignorance was off-putting. My decision not to read as much has resulted in a newfound ability to reach within, and think for myself, rather than being influenced by the thoughts of others who are part of an industry focused on promoting a certain mainstream and ideological-driven worldview.

This journey has brought me to some inconvenient conclusions about topics I spent much of my career working on. The global environmental movement is steeped in western approaches and solutions, which seek to project the idea that it is the west which cares the most, yet they're not willing to pay the price and change their current economic model, which is rooted in promoting relentless consumption. The concept of net-zero is really a westernized approach based on this agenda whereby it is assumed the poor nations will stay poor, and the wealthy countries can continue with their manufacturing and just buy carbon credits and plant some trees in other parts of the world. So reading aside, if I intend to write another book, it would be called 'The Assault of Modernity', about the risks to a world where western ideas dominate due to historical 'mind capture', many of which are not suited to most culture around the world, and which in fact could cause a great deal of social discord and disruption.

LEAPFROGGING

A leapfrog idea to benefit the world would be to get rid of, or vastly reduce, the size of armies around the world and turn them into a labour pool dedicated to improving basic infrastructure. We need a peace industry to replace the military industrial complex. It could actually create many economic benefits, which we mistakenly think can be secured through war. When we consider that most wars are fought because of a desire to control resources, the big leapfrog question is whether it's something the tech industry should be focusing on, to reduce the risk of meaningless wars. That would be true innovation.

**To see more on
Chandran Nair**

GRATITUDE

I want to thank my wife, my two children and my parents

BECOME A PART OF THE MOVEMENT

www.theartofleapfrogging.com

Printed in Great Britain
by Amazon